THE QI ANNUAL

'F'

Edited by John Lloyd and John Mitchinson

Art Direction by David Costa

A Birthday FFib

*There was only ever one Faber – Geoffrey – who founded the publishing house Faber & Gwyer in 1925.
When he bought out Lady Gwyer's stake in 1929, the poet Walter de la Mare suggested he add a second fictional
Faber because it sounded good and 'you can't have enough of a good thing'.
And so it has proved. Happy 80th Faber!*

ff

faber and faber

Other books from QI

The Book of General Ignorance
The Book of General Ignorance: Pocket Edition
The Book of Animal Ignorance
The QI 'E' Annual
Advanced Banter: The QI Book of Quotations
The Sound of General Ignorance

First published in 2008
by Faber and Faber Limited
3 Queen Square London WC1N 3AU

Printed in Italy by L.E.G.O. S.p.A.

A CIP record for this book
is available from the British Library

ISBN 978–0–571–24414–0

2 4 6 8 10 9 7 5 3

CONTENTS

fun

FRANKS in FLIGHT

Throughout history men called Frank have been at the forefront of Man's eternal quest to conquer the skies...

In 1910, pioneering American pilot **FRANK COFFYN** was granted his wings by non-other than Wilbur Wright. Frank became a regular member of the Wright brothers' exhibition flying team, and in 1912 he flew a Wright Model B plane above New York City. He thrilled the thousands of onlookers by swooping down and flying beneath the Brooklyn and Williamsburg bridges. Coffyn is credited with having taken the first aerial photographs of New York city. He became an army flying instructor during World War I, and later in life he qualified as a helicopter pilot.

On June 2nd 1933, record-breaking US aviator **FRANK HAWKS** set a new trans-continental airspeed record when he flew his Northrop Gamma non-stop from Los Angeles to New York in 13 hours, 26 minutes and 15 seconds. Hawks was the man who introduced Amelia Earhart (right) to flying when, on 28th December 1920, he took her for a ten minute flight at Long Beach, California. In 1932 Earhart became the first woman to fly solo across the Atlantic. She died in 1937, when her plane vanished during an attempt to circumnavigate the globe. Frank Hawks died the following year, when his Gwinn Aircar hit telephone wires shortly after take-off at East Aurora, New York.

Balloon busting **FRANK LUKE** was America's second highest scoring air ace during World War I, destroying 18 enemy aircraft in one frantic spell between September 12th and 29th, 1918. A hot-headed former bare-knuckle boxer, he was disliked by some of his colleagues for his aggressive nature and tendency to fly alone. His luck ran out when he was shot down over enemy lines near Murveaux in France. Despite having been wounded in the shoulder by anti-aircraft fire, Luke drew his pistol and shot dead a further 7 German soldiers before he himself was shot and killed. In 1921 Frank Luke was awarded a posthumous US Medal of Honor for his act of heroism.

Squadron Leader 'Fearless' **FRANK DAY** lost a thumb and was shot in the knee when his Spitfire was downed off the coast of Crete in 1942. After 24 hours in the water, Day was rescued by an enemy ship, and sent to the notorious Stalag Luft III POW camp, scene of the real-life 'Great Escape'.

Frank acted as a 'penguin', dispersing spoil from the escape tunnel in his trouser legs. Another claim to fame was that in 1938, whilst serving as an RAF flying instructor, Frank taught Kiang Chai-shek to fly. His pupil later became the first president of the Communist Chinese republic.

On February 6th 1958, a plane carrying Manchester United back from a European Cup tie against Red Star Belgrade crashed during take-off at Munich airport. The only Frank to perish in the disaster was **FRANK SWIFT**. Ironically, Swift made all of his 338 football league appearances for United's arch-rivals Manchester City. Having retired in 1949, he was working as a reporter for the *News of the World* when disaster struck.

FEB 6th 1958

MUNICH

WILLS CIGARETTES

FRANKS IN FLIGHT

Teenage fraudster **FRANK ABAGNALE** flew over 1,000,000 miles on over 250 Pan-Am flights, visiting 26 different countries, without paying for a single ticket. He simply posed as an airline pilot travelling between jobs. As well as free flights, all Frank's hotel expenses were charged to Pan-Am. In the movie *Catch Me If You Can* Frank's character was played by Leonardo DiCaprio.

FRANKS in SPACE

FRANK BORMAN was Mission Commander of Apollo 8, Man's first expedition to the Moon. He spent Christmas 1968 in orbit above the lunar surface.

FRANK CULBERTSON was Commander of the International Space Station in 2001. On 9/11 he was the only American not on Earth when the Twin Towers were attacked.

FRANCO MALERBA was the first Italian in space. Despite looking alarmingly like Captain Black (evil opponent of indestructible TV space puppet Captain Scarlet) Malerba was chosen to serve as payload specialist on board a Space Shuttle mission in the summer of 1992. Fortunately there was no reported contact with the Mysterons during the flight. Back in the 1970s while carrying out post-graduate research, Malberba conducted a series of experiments using the eyeballs of frogs.

FRANK HAMPSON travelled further in space than any other Frank, albeit in his imagination. He created legendary *Pilot of the Future* Dan Dare, who first appeared in the *Eagle* comic in 1950. *Eagle* was founded by Rev. Marcus Morris, a vicar from Southport, Lancashire, who believed that American comics were having a bad influence on British boys.

Come fly with Frank

FRANK SINATRA owned a string of aeroplanes, one of which was *Christina II*, the 1965 Lear jet in which the crooner wooed Mia Farrow. He loaned his sleek passion wagon to Elvis and Priscilla Presley for their honeymoon, and in 2 years Frank and his Rat Pack pals clocked up 1500 hours of flying time in the 500mph jet. In 1977 Sinatra's mother 'Dolly' died when a Lear jet she was travelling in crashed on San Gorgonio mountain, California. She had been heading for Las Vegas to see her son perform.

'Frank' was not a popular name among allied pilots in the Pacific during WWII. For that was the code name given to the Imperial Japanese Army's powerful Nakajima Ki-84 *Hayate* single seat fighter, of which over 3,500 examples were produced, commencing in 1943.

Sir FRANK WHITTLE did more to further Man's aerial ambition than any other Frank. As any 1950s schoolboy will tell you, Sir Frank Whittle invented the jet engine. Actually he *co-invented* it, as German boffin Hans von Ohain was busily inventing it at exactly the same time. Frank's first jet propelled prototype got off the ground on April 7th 1941. Hans had managed to get his first effort airborne 5 days earlier. A big bronze statue of Sir Frank, looking closely at his thumb, was unveiled in Coventry on June 1st 2007, on what would have been his 100th birthday. He died in 1996.

Maintaining the great tradition of Franks in Flight is American **FRANK PRELL** who, for reasons best known to himself, maintains a collection of ridiculous hot air balloons, including this one - in the shape of a giant birthday cake.

G-BZNZ

9

The Qi

CUP FINAL

THE QI CUP FINAL
The most interesting game of football sadly never played, in which Stephen's effortless aristos and brainboxes take on Alan's naturally gifted squad of backstreet heroes.

FRY's GENTLEMEN'S XI

Goal Keeper: Niels Bohr (1885-1962)
Some say that Nobel Prize winner Bohr played internationally for Denmark and that Albert Camus played for Algeria, but in fact they're wrong: neither ever represented their country. Niels Bohr once let in an outrageously long shot due to being distracted by a mathematical problem, while Camus once claimed 'All I know most surely about morality and obligations, I owe to football.'

Left Back: C.B. Fry (1872-1956)
As well as being one of the greatest English cricketers of all time and a holder of the world long jump record, Fry was a full back for England, Southampton, Portsmouth and Corinthians (a team of such sportsmen that they deliberately missed penalties, refusing to believe the other team had meant to foul them). One of Fry's party pieces was to jump backwards from the floor onto a mantelpiece.

Centre Back: Max Woosnam (1892-1965)

Cambridge University's Max Woosnam fought alongside Siegfried Sassoon in WWI and once beat Charlie Chaplin at table tennis using a butter knife instead of a bat. He played football for Chelsea, Man City and England as well as winning a gold medal in tennis at the 1920 Olympics. Woosnam was also on the board of ICI and drove a bus during the General Strike of 1926.

Centre Back: Henry VIII (1491-1547)

The first known pair of football boots were catalogued in Henry VIII's possessions when he died. Although he once banned the game, this certainly implies that he played it, and while we don't know of his preferred position, his ample frame would surely complement Woosnam's natural ability in the centre of defence.

Right Back: Arthur Conan Doyle (1859-1930)

Arthur Conan Doyle was a keen sportsman, a founder member of Portsmouth FC and the team's first ever goalkeeper. 'Pompey' (Sherlock Holmes himself would struggle to pick the right origin for this nickname - there are *at least* 8 different theories) were very successful in their first season, only losing 3 of their first 22 games, and beating the Royal Marines 10-0.

Left Midfield: Cuthbert Ottaway (1850-1878)

Cuthbert Ottaway was the first ever captain of the England football team. Educated at Eton, he also played cricket for England. In those days, footballing skills didn't stretch to passing: players would just dribble with the ball until they got tackled. Ottaway was the epitome of elegance on and off the field. A barrister, he died at the age of 27 from a chill caught in the course of a night's dancing.

Right Midfield: al-Saadi Gaddafi (1973-)

The son of Libya's leader often benefited from somewhat dubious refereeing decisions. His position of captain of the Libyan football team was helped by his position as president of the Libyan football federation. A move to play in Italy was ill-fated. Gaddafi played only one game for Perugia before failing a drugs test; he was once trained by the disgraced Canadian athlete Ben Johnson.

Central Midfield: Sócrates (1954-)

Brazilian legend Sócrates Brasileiro Sampaio de Souza Vieira de Oliveira, better known simply as Sócrates, earned his degree in medicine while simultaneously playing professional football. Sócrates was also a political activist, co-founding the Corinthian Democracy, an ideological movement that helped overthrow Brazil's military dictatorship in 1982.

Attacker: Simen Agdestein (1967-)

Simen Agdestein played professional football for Norway, and is perhaps the only person in the world to be an international footballer and a chess grandmaster. Though he has not yet broken into the world elite, he was Norwegian champion at 15, a grandmaster at 18, and came second at the 1986 World Junior Chess Championships.

Attacker: Alfred Lyttelton (1857-1913)

Yet another Etonian, Alfred Lyttelton was the *first* man to represent England at both football and cricket. He went on to become a liberal MP and was president of the MCC. In 1900 he was sent to South Africa to oversee the country's reconstruction after the Boer War, and was an advocate of women's suffrage. Alfred Lyttelton was the great-uncle of *I'm Sorry I Haven't A Clue*'s late great Humphrey.

Attacker: Luther Blissett (1958-)

According to football folklore, England international Luther Blissett only got to sign for AC Milan because they mistook him for John Barnes. He has had the last laugh, though, as the inspiration for the 'Luther Blissett Project', a collection of anonymous Italian *avant garde* artists whose manifesto states: 'Anyone can be Luther Blissett simply by adopting the name.' Blissett himself is a member.

DAVIES's Players' XI

Central Midfield: Milene Domingues (1979-)
The only woman (and Buddhist) in the team, Domingues is a former model and the ex-wife of Brazilian striker Ronaldo who first saw her on TV practising her ball-juggling skills (aged 17, she set a new world record of 55,187 keepy-uppies). She currently plays for Italian team Fiamma Monza — her £200K transfer in 2002 made her the most expensive woman player ever.

Central Midfield: Diego Maradona (1960-1997)
Maradona is the only member of the Players' XI to have a religion named after him; the Church of Maradona has over 80,000 worshippers. Maradona has been suspended twice for drug abuse and once opened fire with an air rifle on journalists. Now a successful television presenter, he is one the few talk-show hosts to have interviewed his hero, Fidel Castro (he has his portrait tattooed on his leg).

Attacker: Héctor Castro (1904-1960)
Uruguayan international Héctor Castro scored the winning goal in the first ever World Cup final in 1930 in Montevideo. He remains the only one-armed person to have achieved this. Known as 'el Manco', the 13-year-old Castro accidentally amputated his right forearm with an electric saw. It didn't hold him back: he used his stump as a club when leaping for headers and had a reputation as a serious womaniser.

Attacker: Eduard Streltsov (1937-1990)
Eduard Streltsov was known as the Russian Pelé. His loyalty to Torpedo Moscow meant he refused to join either the Army's CSKA Moscow or the KGB's Dynamo Moscow. As a result, he was accused of rape and sent to work in the Siberian Gulag for seven years. When he returned, commentators noted that he had lost a few yards of pace, but still led Torpedo to the Russian championship.

Goalkeeper: William Foulkes (1874-1916)
William 'Fatty' Foulkes was a 25 stone keeper for England, Sheffield United, Bradford City and Chelsea; he also played cricket for Derbyshire. It took six men to carry him off the field when he was injured. Once when playing Liverpool, he picked up their centre forward, turned him upside down and planted him in the mud.

Left Back: Jesper Olsen (1961-)
Perhaps more of a left winger, but Olsen takes his place in our back four thanks to a terrible defensive pass in the 1986 World Cup in Denmark's game against Spain which allowed Emilío Butragueño to score and has since made Olsen's name synonymous with error. 'Rigtig Jesper Olsen' (a right Jesper Olsen) is now Danish slang for a gaffe of any kind.

Right Back: Billy Meredith (1874-1958)
Meredith played for Manchester Utd and Wales at the turn of the 20th century, but began his working life driving pit ponies. He was instrumental in setting up the first footballers' union. Banned for 10 years for allegedly bribing an opposition player, Meredith liked to chew tobacco 'for concentration'. He changed to chewing toothpicks after the cleaners refused to wash his tobacco-stained shirts.

Centre Back: Jah Bless Youth (c 1981-)
The Players' XI answer to Mr Fry's polymaths, Jah Bless Youth is not only a professional footballer – playing in the heady heights of the Swiss and Irish 3rd divisions – he is also a reggae-ragga-ska-dub rapper and drummer. His music aims to bring the 'message of the Almighty' to the younger generation. He has released four albums including 2004's *Babylon Stop Abusing Human Kind*.

Centre Back: Charlie Oatway (1973-)
The former Brentford and Brighton defender is actually called Anthony Philip David Terry Frank Donald Stanley Gerry Gordon Stephen James Oatway – he is named after the QPR's entire 1973 first-team squad. He is called 'Charlie' because when his parents told his aunt the proposed name, she said 'he'd look a right Charlie', and the name stuck.

Left Midfield: José Moreno (1916-1978)
No, not Jose Mourinho. Known as *El Charro* (the cowboy), this Argentinian legend played for River Plate in the 1940s and was famous for his unusual training regime. He believed the best possible training for a football match was to dance the tango until late and then bed a couple of women. For lunch before kick-off, he would eat chicken stew and drink a bottle or three of red wine.

Right Midfield: Garrincha (1933-1983)
According to his biography by Ruy Castro, the well-hung Brazilian legend lost his virginity to a goat. One of his legs was two inches shorter than the other, which gave him a distinctive gait; hence 'Garrincha,' meaning 'little bird'. He never trained, and once stored the cash bonus from a World Cup win in a mattress, only to find some years later it had rotted due to his child wetting the bed.

THE F ARCHIPELAGO

Fugloy easternmost of the Faroe Islands, means 'bird Island' in Faroese. It has one road, no trees, 200,000 puffins and a mountain called Klubbin. No one is quite sure about how many people live there: the official records say 44, but that doesn't include the huldufolk or 'other people' who lead a parallel existence but cannot be seen unless they choose to be. It is also supposed to be full of trolls (or trølls, as they are called in Faroese). It would be a good place to lie low if you practised the dark arts: the Faroes are the only country in Northern Europe never to have burned a witch.

Fernando Póo part of the former Spanish colony of Equatorial Guinea (now the richest country in Africa), is named after the Portuguese explorer who first charted it in 1472. He himself called it Formosa ('beautiful'), a name also later given to Taiwan by another Portuguese in 1544. In 1973, the dictator of Equatorial Guinea renamed the island Masie Nguema Biyogo after himself: since his overthrow in 1979 it has been called Bioko. One of Nguema's many crimes took place in the island's football stadium in 1973, where 150 alleged conspirators were put to death as speakers blasted out the President's favourite song, *Those Were the Days* by winsome Welsh songstress, Mary Hopkin. The main residents of Fernando Póo are the Bubi people, also called the Bube, the Boombe, the Ibubi and the eVoové. Their name for the island is Otcho.

Fiji consists of 322 islands set in 129,500 sq km (50,000 sq miles) of the Pacific. This is an area larger than Britain, France and Spain combined, but only 1.5% of it is land. Most Fijians live on Viti Levu. When warning Captain Cook of the ferocity of their neighbours, the Tongans mispronounced Viti as Fisi and the name stuck. Hairdressing and human flesh played major roles in traditional Fijian society. To touch a chief's hair was to invite certain death, as English missionary Rev. Thomas Baker found out in 1867 in a misunderstanding over a comb. He was the only missionary to be eaten on Fiji but there is evidence that human flesh was consumed just because it was delicious – the best bits being thigh, heart and bicep.

Fogo Island off Newfoundland is one of the four corners of the earth according to the Flat Earth Society. It is so isolated its main settlement is called Seldom-Come-By and many residents still speak in an Elizabethan dialect. It was once home to the Beothuk people, the original 'Red Indians' – so called not for their skin colour, but the red ochre they rubbed all over themselves and their possessions. Their campfires gave the island its name: fogo is Portuguese for fire – also the source of the name of the other Fogo, a 3,000 m (9,842 ft) marine volcano and the hottest of the Cape Verde Islands.

Flores east of Java in Indonesia, was once home to a hobbit-like race called *Homo floresiensis*, who were 90 cm (3 ft) tall with heads the size of grapefruit. They survived until 11,000 years ago, making sophisticated stone tools to hunt the miniature elephants or stegodons that also lived on the island – and the Flores giant rat, which is the size of a terrier. Today, the local Nage tribe still tell tales of the ebu gogo: tiny, hairy, pot-bellied humans who lived in the jungle and could be heard muttering to themselves in a strange language. Flores is also home to the word's largest and nastiest lizard, the komodo dragon, whose existence had been written off as a myth by western science until its discovery in 1912.

Ferdinandea off the coast of Sicily, is only visible above sea level if it's erupting and, when it does emerge, it causes territorial disputes. In 1831, four different countries (including Britain) claimed it, but it re-submerged a year later before the issue of its sovereignty could be resolved. In 1986, with its summit only a couple of metres below the sea, a US Air Force plane on the way to Tripoli bombed it after the pilot mistook it for a Libyan submarine.

Foula in Shetland, is Britain's most northerly inhabited island and the possible location of the mythical Ultima Thule, the classical name for the end of the known world (reputedly made from a substance with the consistency of jellyfish). It is the last place in Europe still to use the Julian calendar, dropped by the rest of Britain in 1752: Christmas on Foula is on our 6th January, New Year's Day on 13th January. Foula means 'Bird Island' in Old Norse and it is home to the world's largest colony of Great Skuas, locally known as 'bonxies'.

15

FINANCE
101 Uses For a Dead Hedge Fund Manager...

no. 4

no. 17

no. 31

no. 35

no. 42

no. 59

no. 63

no. 75

no. 82

no. 87

no. 94

no. 101

YE FRAUDULENTE HISTORIE OF FAKENHAM

Fakenham is an ancient Saxon town in Norfolk, mentioned in the 'Domesday Book'. It became famous in the 1990s when it was widely described in the national newspapers as 'the most boring place on earth'. That was not true*, and nothing else on this page is true either. Apart from this bit, of course.

One of the earliest known sex-change operations nears its grisly conclusion.

Turbulent seas during the Roman occupation caused a pasta supplies ship to sink off the north Norfolk coast some nine miles from Fakenham. For almost a year afterwards, ships had great difficulty navigating the Vermicelli Straits.

Novice Agnes Queate pummelling Slime Tuber, a kind of acidic parsnip, to a mulch. Widely used as a shaving balm by penitent monks at the Abbey.

Inigo Thucke, a pioneer of selective breeding programmes, demonstrates his flock of micro-sheep. These tiny animals proved very popular with the gentry of Fakenham for the sweetness of their meat and the fact that they would fit inside a bun. Just visible in the background is Thucke's extraordinary floating goat that was propelled skywards by bodily gas emissions. Sadly, the animal exploded over Little Snoring and Inigo was so depressed he never bred another.

Dark Days – The fear of witches was taken to bloody extremes during the Fakenham Assizes of 1646-50, when almost any physical deformity was treated as a sure sign of Demonic affiliation. In one notable incident, the artist Enoch Butters was hanged as a witch merely for having an excessively pointy chin.

Gathering in the Fakenham hemp harvest often had a soporific and, occasionally, aphrodisiac effect upon the reapers. The harvest was often delayed for several days because of amorous mishaps - leading, nine months later, to the arrival of so-called 'Hash-a-bye Babies'.

Dr Napkin's free school. Napkin advocated that students should be free to express themselves in any way they felt appropriate. Here we see a small group of pupils expressing themselves by planning to sear the doctor's backside with a cattle brand while his dog is forced to eat a skunk's tail.

Warwick Soyle takes the stand to defend himself against the charge that he has made the crappiest desk in history.

*The error arose from the fact that a single contributor to the internet site The Knowhere Guide (www.knowhere.co.uk) had described Wednesday afternoons in Fakenham (early closing) as 'the most boring place on earth'. This was taken out of context and Fakenham hit the national headlines as 'having been voted the most boring place on earth', causing the town council considerable expenditure of time and money trying to prove otherwise. Current attractions in Fakenham include The Museum of Gas and Local History, which is open every Thursday.

FIFTEEN FINLAND FACTS

The statements below are all absolutely true. Finland is the most truthful place on earth*.

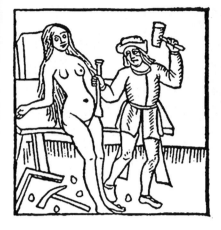

1. It is polite to remove shoes when entering a Finnish home.
2. St Henry, patron saint of Finland, was neither Finnish nor a saint.

3. A third of Finland is covered in peat.
4. In the 17th and 18th centuries, Finland's major export was tar.

5. Only three of the lakes in Finland are more than 91m (300 ft) deep.
6. Local handicrafts include making wooden reindeer-milking bowls.

7. Finland is the world's largest producer of farm-raised foxes.
8. The log cabin was invented in Finland.

9. Helsinki is the smallest city in the world ever to host the Olympic Games.
10. The last Peasant's Revolt in Europe took place in Finland in 1596-7.

11. The World Air Guitar Championships are held annually in Oulu, Finland.

12. There are some two million saunas in Finland. Almost every building in the country has at least one.
13. The second-largest religion in the country is the Finnish Greek Orthodox Church, which reports to the Bishop of Constantinople.

14. The maximum number of reindeer permitted by law in Finland is 224,900.
15. Swedish is compulsory in Finnish schools but most Finns never really learn to speak it properly.

*Finland is officially the world's least corrupt country. Transparency International, a Berlin-based research group, produces an annual Corruption Perception Index, grading every nation state. In the 2007 report, Finland was narrowly beaten to the top spot by Denmark - with New Zealand coming third, the UK 12th and the USA 20th. But this is an aberration. Finland has consistently won the poll since the millennium, coming top in 2001, 2002, 2003, 2004 and 2006 with another second place in 2005 (won by Iceland). The bottom four in 2007 were: Haiti, Iraq, Burma (Myanmar) and Somalia (judged the world's most corrupt state).

FROG SALAD

DECLARE A GREEN ALERT!

The world is losing its frogs. A third of the 5,250 recorded species are threatened with extinction through disease and climate change; since the 1950s at least 120 species have already joined the great froggy chorus in the sky. This must stop.

HERE ARE FOURTEEN REASONS WHY.

1. Glass Frogs, or Ghost Frogs, are lime green on top, but translucent below. Get underneath one and you can see its heart beating, its skeleton and its intestines. Why? Is this an evolved defence against dissection by biology students?

2. Bion, a popular philosopher of Athens, born around 325 BC, wrote: 'Boys throw stones at frogs for fun, but the frogs don't die for fun, but in sober earnest.' But it's hard to imagine a sober earnest frog, alive or dead. Look ...

3. *Pipa pipa* is the Surinam Toad from South America. It looks like a pancake. For three centuries after it was discovered, no one knew how it reproduced. *Pipa pipa* knew. The male and female perform a simultaneous underwater somersault, at the peak of which the female lays eggs which fall onto the male's belly. During the descent, the male fertilises the eggs and presses them upon the female's honeycombed back. Over and over, they somersault. Once she has about 100 fertilised eggs on her back, her skin swells up and envelops them. Months later, she moults her skin and fully formed tiny toads emerge.

4. All toads are frogs. Not all are Surinams. In some species, it is almost physically impossible to separate a mating pair, so solid is their embrace. They will part when they are ready. Leave them be, can't you?

5. But frogs have never been let be.
The Florida Department of Agriculture, in 1952, published 50 recipes for bullfrog meat, including:
Bullfrog Pot Pie
Bullfrog à la King
Bullfrog Shortcakes
Bullfrog Omelette
Bullfrog Clubhouse Sandwich
French Toasted Bullfrog, and ...

Bullfrog Salad.

6. In the Middle Ages, great houses employed servants whose sole job was to interrupt the brouhaha of croaking frogs by throwing stones into ponds all night, so that their masters might sleep.

7. The Northern Pool Frog croaks in a Norfolk accent. It went extinct in England in the 1990s, but was re-introduced into the Fens in 2005. From Sweden.

8. In Windham, Connecticut, in 1754, the people waited trembling for war to reach their village bournes. One steamy midnight in June, a deafening tumult of hatred and terror woke them all, and sent them screaming from their beds. The Day of Judgement, or Indians attacking? Either way, the villagers ran. In the morning light, they returned and found their foe: thousands of bullfrogs, drawn to a local pond by a freak drought.

9. Not all frogs sing chorally. Spring Peeper Frogs form trios: one frog plays an A; a second soon responds in G sharp; after a while of this duetting, a third frog joins in with a B. And so it goes on: A, G sharp, B ... A, G sharp, B ... Even if part of a gathering of hundreds, each Peeper ignores the songs of all the others, only responding to the members of its own combo.

10. Frogs, like birds, communicate with songs instead of smells. The song of the American Toad reminds many of the opening movement of Beethoven's 'Moonlight Sonata'. The Colorado River Toad's call resembles a ferryboat whistle. Others sound like pigs, like hounds or squirrels, like two carpenters banging in nails out of synch. The distress call of the bullfrog is endlessly mistaken for a human scream. And not only in Connecticut.

11. Green Tree Frogs have been known to respond to sounds other than Green Tree Frog calls, including the mating calls of washing machines, popcorn makers, car alarms, and the cannons roaring in a film about the US Civil War.

12. Sometimes, in mass mating sessions triggered by sudden downpours, male toads will attempt to mount other males. The male underneath gives a harsh, high-pitched croak of protest, repeatedly, until the one on top gets off. This is the most commonly heard of all toad calls, which must tell you something.

13. In many lands, frogs are good luck symbols. In Japan especially, the bullfrog is propitious, being descended from a fabled ancestor capable of sucking all the mosquitoes out of a room with one mighty inhalation.

14. 2008 is the official International Year of the Frog.

And also International Year of the Potato.

And of Sanitation.

And of The Planet Earth.

And of Astronomy, and of the Coral Reef, and of Languages.

But mostly, surely, of the Frog.

There are over 100,000 species of **fungi** and 250,000 known species of **flowering plant**. The **flower auction** at Aalsmeer in the Netherlands is largest in the world: 19 million **flowers** pass through its halls every day. The '**Flower of Kent**' is a large green-skinned variety of apple, thought to h been the one that inspired Sir Isaac Newton to **formulate** his theory of gravity. There are about 12,000 known species of **fern**. **Ferns** range in size the tiny **fragile** *Ophioglossaceae* that produce just one **frond** a year and the **filmy ferns** *Hymenophyliaceae* whose **fronds** are only one or two thick, to the monstrous triffids in the genus *Cyathea* that have stems like tree trunks and can grow up to 80 feet (24m) tall. **Ferns** have more chromoso than any other living thing. The '**futhork**' or '**futhark**' is the Runic alphabet, named after its first six letters f, u, th, o or a, r and k. In the year 2000, a 185,000 **foetuses** were aborted in Britain – more than 3,500 a week. You are 20 times more likely to be involved in a **fatal car accident** in the T World than in Europe. The last **fatality** caused by an adder sting in Britain was a **five-year old girl** in 1977. A **fatal dose** of chocolate for a human b is about 10kg (22lb) and for a dog about 2kg. A small songbird can succumb to a single Smartie. Birds are **feathered reptiles**. The **fear of feather** called pteronophobia. Xenophon of Kos, personal physician of the Emperor Claudius, murdered his patient by sticking a poisoned **feather** down his thr The **faster** a bird runs, the **fewer** toes it has. No bird has more than **four toes** on each **foot**. The abalone is a huge marine snail that has only one – though this accounts for two-thirds of its body weight. Andorra is the only country in the world with a **free postal service**. PETA, the **fundamenta animal rights** group, claims that cows can suffer from humiliation if people laugh at them. There are **fourteen** species of crocodile. **Flore Nightingale** owned 60 cats. Before the banning of **fox hunting** in Britain, an average 16,000 **foxes** were killed by hunts each year, compared with are 300,000 **foxes** that died of natural causes or in road accidents. Hitler banned **fox hunting** in Germany because he thought it was cruel and immora Siberia in 1623, a single black **fox-fur** pelt could be exchanged for a cabin with **fifty** acres of land, **five** horses, ten cows and twenty sheep. Horses v originally hunted for **food**. The largest **food company** in the world is Nestlé SA of Switzerland. Modern Americans spend more money on **fast food** on higher education, personal computers, computer software or new cars. A single potato crisp production line uses in one hour as many potatoe could be planted, grown and harvested from a **full-size football pitch**. Robert Mitchum could memorise his lines from an entire **film script** after a si read-through. He chose most of his **films** on the basis of how much time off he could get to go **fishing**. The greatest depth at which a **fish** has caught is 27,200 feet (8,370m). **Fishermen** kill about 100,000 albatrosses a year. They die on the baited hooks of **fishing lines** that can be up to 80 r long. **Forty-three** per cent of British 7 year olds do not understand the word 'amber'. Amber is the **fossilised resin** of pine trees. Wombats have cu shaped **faeces**. St **Fidelis** of Sigmarigen's skull is buried in **Feldkirch**, Austria but the rest of him is buried in Chur, Switzerland. **Four million peo** visit the tomb of St **Francis of Assisi** every year. Gabriele **Falloppio** (1523-62), also known as **Fallopius**, was the **first man** to describe the clitori to name the vagina. Though he described the **Fallopian tubes** that are named after him, he was not the **first to do so** and didn't understand what were for. He called them 'the trumpets of the uterus'. **Fromology** is the study of cheese. Aerodontia is the branch of dentistry dealing with probl caused by **flying**. In Croatia, so many may**flies** hatch on the rivers that **farmers** scrape them off the surface and use them as **fertiliser**. There are r than **forty** different ethnic groups in Gabon, but one third of the population belong to the **Fang** tribe. The **Fang** are the only ethnic group in Gabon have always opposed slavery. The lovely stained glass windows in the Süleymaniye Mosque in Istanbul were crafted by the **famous glazier** Ibrahim Drunkard. According to Canadian scientists, winning an Oscar extends an actor's life by **four years**: winning two Oscars by six. Crickets have their on their **forelegs**. Bhutan and Nepal are the only two countries in the world where **female life expectancy** is less than the male. Admiral of the F Lord 'Jackie' **Fisher** (1841-1920), the **First Sea Lord**, sent his **favourite niece** £10 in cash for her wedding, accompanied by a note saying he w never speak to her again because she was marrying an Army officer. The **flag of Liechtenstein** had a crown put on it in 1937, to distinguish it from **flag of Haiti**. Modern Haiti is one of the **four most corrupt countries** in the world. One of principal exports of Liechtenstein is **false teeth**. The **name** of the novelist F. **Scott Fitzgerald** (1896-1940) was **Francis Scott Key Fitzgerald**: he was named after his second cousin three times remo **Francis Scott Key**, author of *The Star Spangled Banner*. The real name of the novelist **Ford Madox Ford** (1873-1939) was **Ford Hermann Hue** Robert **FitzRoy**, captain of the *Beagle* (on which Darwin **first formulated** the Theory of Evolution) was the inventor of weather **forecasting**. Otto Ro **Frisch** (1904-79), an Austrian physicist sacked by Hitler from Hamburg University for being Jewish in 1933, went on to conceive the atomic bomb. **Haber** (1868-1934) invented chemical warfare in Germany during the **First World War**. He called it 'a higher **form of killing**'. After the war, he esca to Switzerland in a **false beard**. In 1918, he was awarded the Nobel Prize for Chemistry. **Friedrich** Wilhelm Heinrich Alexander von Humboldt (1 1859) is said to have been the last man in history who knew everything that could be known. Thomas Jefferson (1743-1826), 3rd President of the Un States, invented the **foldaway bed**. In her **final movie**, made in her mid-80s, Mae West remained convinced she was a sex symbol, even though was nearly blind, stone deaf and so elderly that, when she had to turn round on camera, a stage hand crouching out of shot would swivel her by ankles. W.C. **Fields** called her 'a plumber's idea of Cleopatra'. The names Honda and Toyota both come from Japanese words meaning '**field of ri** Honda means 'main rice **field**' and Toyota means 'abundant rice **field**'. In 'Cow Bingo', a **field** is divided into squares that players can 'buy'. A cow i into the **field**, and the player on whose square the **first cowpat** lands wins. **Fair Isle**, lying between the Orkneys and the Shetlands, is Britain's remo inhabited island. The **Faroe Islands** are **famous** for fog. On Mykines, it is **foggy** for 100 days a year. **Faroe islanders** claim that it is possibl experience all **four seasons** in a single day. The name **Funchal**, the capital of the island of Madeira, comes from the Portuguese for **fennel**. The G for **fennel** is 'marathon'. Only 100 people in the world are **fluent** in Cornish. The last person to speak Cornish as their **first language** was Dolly Pentr of Mousehole, who died in 1777. There are **four hundred and twenty-seven thousand villages** in India. The world's most **fertile bull**, Itofuku died in Japan in January 2002. In a 20-year career, he **fathered** 39,157 calves, averaging over **forty-nine** a week. The Kalashnikov is the most wi used **firearm** in the world, more than **fifty** national armies have them in their arsenal. A bullet **fired** from a Kalashnikov weighs only a quarter o ounce, but leaves the barrel at over 1,500 mph. This gives it a **force of impact** equivalent to that of a brick dropped from the top of St Paul's Cathe **Falling coconuts** kill 150 people a year, ten times as many people as are killed by sharks. Henry **Ford**, William Durant (founder of General Mot Ettore Bugatti and Louis Delage all died in 1947, the year that **Ferrari** was founded. Carrara in Italy is the source of the world's most **famous marb** is so plentiful that it is ground into sand for use in concrete. The town is almost as **famous** for salted, aged and spiced pig **fat** or lard, a Tuscan delic The **finest lard** - sometimes called leaf lard - comes from inside the loin and around the kidneys of a pig. This kind of pig **fat** is called the **flare**. Accor to leading redneck authority Jeff **Foxworthy**, you may be a redneck if you have ever used lard in bed. All **fats** are composed of crystals. Most crys have an irregular shape, but the angle between their **facets** always remains constant. The German for **fat** is Schmalz. **Faggots** are a kind of ch sausage made with pork offal mixed with **fat**, breadcrumbs and onions. An accident with a batch of **faggots** started the Great **Fire of London** in Pud Lane in 1666. Each year, up to 200 million tons of Chinese coal bursts into **flames** whilst still underground. There are at least 60 such **fires** ragir China at this moment. One of them, at Baijigou in northwest China, has been on **fire** continuously for 150 years. Such **fires** produce more greenho gases than all the cars in Germany put together. Golf was played in ancient China, more than **five hundred years** before it was first mentione Scotland. The **first recorded** mention of golf in Scotland, in 1457, made it a **felony**, punishable by death. During his lifetime, Benny Hill was the n **famous comedian** in the world. His biggest **fan** was Charlie Chaplin. He died at home alone watching television, his body undiscovered for two d The composer Rimsky-Korsakov (1844-1908) was a **full-time naval officer**. Thirty-six per cent of the EU is **forested**, compared to only 8.4% of Bri The world's largest protected **forest** is the Amana Reserve in Brazil. It covers 2,350,000 hectares (9,180 square miles), an area about the size of Belg Technically speaking, an *idiot* is someone with the lowest possible grade of **feeble-mindedness**, having an IQ of less than 25, or a mental age of When Liverpool **footballer** Ian Rush was signed to Juventus and was asked how he **found** living in Italy, he said it was 'like being in a **foreign coun** Since the year 2000, the **Federal Aviation Administration** can propose **fines** of up to $25,000 for unruly passengers. A single incident can resu multiple violations. There are **forty-four** muscles in the human **face**, enabling us to make more than 250,000 different **facial expressions**. The M word *bongking* means 'sprawling **face down** with one's bottom in the air'; *jeremak* means 'suddenly **face to face**'; and *jeremus* means 'to spraw one's **face**'. It is impossible to **faint** while lying down. It's **fascinating** that there are words for the **fear of dust**, clocks or hearing good news, but r for the common ones such as the **fear of school**, bats or bears. Arthur Conan Doyle and W.B. Yeats both believed in **fairies**. **Fairies** are suppose eat copious quantities of weeds. The scientific study of **fingerprints** is called *dermatoglyphics*, a word that has the distinction of being one of the longest in English with no repeated letters. The other one is *uncopyrightable*. The Yiddish for **finger** is 'toe'. **Fireworks** are illegal in Australia. **Faus** is Latin for 'lucky'.

Buteo's Big Box

The idea of building a ship that could carry representatives of every known species has haunted the imagination of scholars and engineers for millennia.

Part of the reason for this is that there are some apparently precise details in the biblical account of the dimensions and methods of construction of Noah's vessel. For example, we know it had a volume of 450,000 cubic cubits, or 1.5 million cubic feet, which is about a third of the volume of the auditorium of the Albert Hall. But arguments have raged about its shape, with most scholars going for the parallelepiped (that's a regular 'box' to you and me). But not the early Christian philosopher Origen (c 185 ~ c 254), who was convinced it was built in the shape of a pyramid, with a base that covered half a square mile. (But then again, he also castrated himself after mis~ reading a passage in the Gospels.)

Probably the most influential attempt to sort out the Ark's logistics was French mathematician Johannes Buteo's *The Shape & Capacity of Noah's Ark*, written in 1554. He proposed that the bottom deck held animals, the middle deck provisions, and the top deck humans and birds ~ as well as dogs (who would be happy eating their own vomit). He imagined the Ark as completely dark on all levels except for the top ~ because 'wild animals and all kind of reptile will actively seek out darkness'. He left the smaller animals such as snakes and lizards out of his plans on the basis that they would 'live in small holes around the stabling and living areas'. And insects were com~ pletely excluded, as they were then thought to be the product of spontaneous generation.

Floating Factory

Buteo thought that the bottom two levels must have holes for animal excrement to fall into the bilge; he also thought that food could be dropped down to the animals from the middle deck, and that water could be passed around the ship through a system of siphons. He envisaged space for the storage of 'agricultural and urban equipment' and 'every kind of workman's tool', factoring in a pantry, kitchen, hand~mills, men's and women's quarters and smokeless logs for fuel. His food store contained a barn filled with every known kind of farmers' crop. He also worked out that the animals' enclosure had to be arranged to ensure their inhabitants stayed in perfect balance to prevent the ship capsizing.

Self~righting

Buteo's work inspired many other 'Ark designers'. The German Jesuit polymath Athanasius Kircher (1601~80) solved the instability problem by keeping the heaviest animals at the bottom of the boat as ballast ~ he used Galileo's research into floating bodies to calculate accurately. His triple~decker contained 50 rooms per deck, housing about 1,000 animals.

Green Herbs, No Ham

And what about the plants themselves? Most are much too delicate to survive a flood ~ maybe Noah could have kept an equivalent of the Doomsday Seed Vault that opened in Svalbard, Norway in February 2008 to preserve 1.5 million agricultural crop seeds.
  As well as crops and seeds, the Ark would also have needed a supply of bamboo: not necessarily for the pandas, who can supplement their diet with insects and fruit, but for bamboo mites and bamboo mealy bugs who live on nothing else. In fact many insects can only feed on certain plants ~ including most of the 6,000 known species of plant~feeding mites.

SURVIVAL KIT

Every Moving Thing that Liveth

So could it be done? For 1,000 animals maybe, but we're now looking at 2 million species, with as many as 30 million more waiting to be named. Taking the lowest reasonable estimate of 5 million species, that's 10 million individual animals to accommodate, or 0.15 cubic feet of space each.

In the world's zoos, there is a ratio of 254 animals per zoo keeper. Noah's family would have had 1.25 million animals each to look after. To feed them all once a day, Noah, his wife, three sons and their wives would have needed to get through 115 animals per second.

But that doesn't begin to solve the feeding problems. A polar bear can eat 50 lb (22.5 kg) of meat at a single sitting, while a walrus is able to eat around 5,000 clams in one meal. The short~nosed fruit bat can eat twice its weight in bananas in three hours (it has the biggest appetite of any mammal for its size). Perhaps Noah fed the carnivores with unicorn, griffin, and the like. That would have helped to keep the food fresh, as well as explaining why those animals haven't survived.

Wood Worriers

Then there are the 3,000 species of termites. It's just possible that the mysterious 'gopher wood', which the Bible claimed the Ark was made from, was cypress pine, which is termite proof ~ but what about teredos, the strange saltwater clams also known as 'shipworms' or 'termites of the sea' that are notorious for devouring wooden hulls? Isambard Kingdom Brunel's engineer father Marc was inspired to build the world's first submarine tunnel (the Thames Tunnel) after watching teredos chomp through cellulose. Solitary confinement would be essential.

Two by Two?

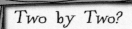

The Ark would also need a 'sexing room', to make sure the right two individuals were selected. It's not as straightforward as it sounds. Male and female hyenas, sea cucumbers, starfish and gila monsters are almost indis~tinguishable without specialist scanning equipment. And what about hermaphrodites, like the 650 known species of leech? Or the Amazonian Molly~fish whose species are all female?

Ordure

Then there's the question of shit. An elephant creates about a tonne of dung per week. Even the 4,500 species of dung beetle are going to have their work cut out chomping through that. A single cow belches about 300 litres of methane a day, along with all the other ruminants, the boat could easily have exploded if subjected to a naked flame. The risk might have been reduced by a giant lightning rod and perhaps a ventilation system powered by the 1,700 species of rodents running around in little wheels.

Odour

And it's not just the dung and the belching: some animals smell bad anyway. Ants were once called 'pismires' due to the urinous odour they give off; skunks smell like rotten eggs mixed with old garlic and burnt rubber and the anal secretion of the ferret~like zorilla can stun a chicken at twenty paces. Perhaps they could bunk up with some of the sweeter smelling denizens: binturongs, for instance, smell of freshly cooked popcorn; tapirs like a crate of lettuce; while koalas eat so much eucalyptus it's easy to mistake them for large furry cough~sweets.

I'm a Patriarch, Get Me Out of Here!

Finally, a year at sea is a long time. Birth control pills would be needed, especially for the 100,000 species of fly, whose descendants can number over 190 trillion within 6 months if left unchecked.

All things considered, it's enough to drive a man to drink. Which is precisely what happened to Noah when the voyage finally ended: 'And Noah began to be an husbandman, and he planted a vineyard: And he drank of the wine, and was drunken; and he was uncovered within his tent.' (Genesis 9:20~21)

After all that stench and sea water, who can blame him?

Illustration: Ted Dewan

French Abuse: Find the Fake French Fraise

As everyone knows, a 'French letter' is slang for a condom and the 'French pox' for venereal disease. For hundreds of years, it has been traditional for the English to ascribe French origins to anything they see as dirty or disgusting.

But can you tell which of the following are real pieces of actual English slang, and which ones have been made up specially for the F Annual?

French abacus
A clitoris

French afternoon
Long lunch followed by sex with a member of staff

French bath
Fellatio

French bathe
To cover oneself in perfume to avoid washing

French bench
A woman's face

French butter
Vaseline

French cannibal
Syphilis

French clock
Cockerel

French cream
Brandy

French culture
Fellatio

French deck
Pornographic playing cards

French dip
Vaginal pre-coital fluid

French dressing
Semen

French Embassy
Any location, such as a gym or YMCA, allowing unbridled homosexual action

French entry
Manhole

French flies
Wasps

French-fried ice-cream
Semen

French girl
Prostitute who specializes in fellatio

French inhale
To blow smoke out through the nose

French job
Fellatio

French lady
Woman who specializes in fellatio but isn't a prostitute.

French lamb
Horse

French language training
Teaching fellatio

French Malteser
Something that won't flush down the lavatory

French marbles
Syphilis

French marriage
Unscheduled sexual encounter
with a total stranger in the toilet on a train

French marzipan
Chicken skin

French measles
Syphilis

French mistress
A female tapir

French muesli
Scabs

French onions
Testicles

French overcoat
Thong

French pig
Syphilis

French plumbing
Violent rattling, thumping and gurgling
coming from next-door's bedroom

French poke
Intimacy with a bar of soap and a radiator

French policeman
Gynaecologist

French polishing
Rubbing oneself between two
ecclesiastical candles

French prints
Unusual heterosexual pornography

French screwdriver
Hammer

French spaghetti house
A brothel that also serves pasta

French towel
Wiping your cock on the curtains

French tricks
Oral sex

French uncle
Milkman

French vanilla
Black term for a sexy white woman

French vowels
The noises made during vigorous homosexual sex

French walk
The posture adopted by someone being thrown out of a
saloon

French wasps
Lisping Italian homosexuals

French window
1. Pants with a rear-entry flap
2. A mirror on the bedroom ceiling

French woman
Fortune-teller

French wrench
Something a plumber has to go and fetch,
allowing him to take an extended lunch
(with sex afterwards)

French yashmak
Panties with a hole in the front

Answers on Page 67

45

FORAGING with SEAN LOCK.

As a moderately successful comedian I often find myself travelling up and down the country performing my humorous routines for the good townsfolk of Britain. Sounds like a good life, and it is. Apart from one thing: <u>food</u>. The only sustenance you can find in the average British city after 10 pm is a kebab or a curry. Eat that for 46 consecutive nights and you'll have a liver the size of a church Bible, no hair, and rickets due to the hours spent in cubicles. You'll be clumsy and slow and have the reflexes of a walrus.

My solution is not a Wild Bean Café or a packed lunch. No, I get out there in the countryside and <u>forage</u>. There are 10,000 species of edible plant in Europe, millions of insects and… mmm…. <u>squirrels</u>.

Coupled with rising food prices, there's never been a better time to put your boots on, march past the supermarket and into the woods.

Here are my DOs and DON'Ts of Foraging

DOs...

Pine needles make good tea.

Birch has a delicious sap you can drink – even more delicious if you've just been drinking pine needle tea.

Acorns and dandelion roots can be roasted for coffee. And if you grind up clover and ivy you get a Decaf Macchiato. (Only joking. What am I like! See how much fun you can have foraging!)

Hen-of-the-Woods fungus smells like mushrooms. And if you know where to find the right kind of mushrooms, it even looks like a hen too.

My favourite is cauliflower fungus. It smells like aniseed and tastes like walnuts. (What more could you want? **Jam on it**.)

The seed cases of wild roses contain more Vitamin C than any other fruit. (And supermarket oranges contain less Vitamin C than slippers.)

Poplar, willow and spruce bark are edible. (NB Look up **edible** in the dictionary before you try them. It doesn't mean 'tasty'…)

Grind insects between two stones and add them to stews. Insects are more nutritious than vegetables and, if you're eating them, they're not crawling up your trouser leg.

Woodlice, starfish, bees and whirligig beetles are all edible. But then so is a pasty from Sandbach Services.

FOREST FEAST

Baby squirrels are delicious! Pluck them from their nests inside hollow trees.

All lizards are edible but do not attempt to eat a Komodo Dragon! (You'll upset the greenies!)

Dazzle frogs at night with a bright light then club them to death. (Not as much fun as it sounds.)

Remember what they say in foraging circles: **'A snake is a steak'**. (It's not, of course: I'd much rather have a steak but it's preferable to a spruce bark wrap and it rhymes.)

Do trap! It requires less skill and leaves more time to forage.

Traps follow these 4 principles. **Mangle, Strangle, Dangle, Tangle.**

A balanced weight MANGLES, a snare STRANGLES, springy saplings whip the prey into the air so they DANGLE, and a net TANGLES.

But don't let it get stuck in your head like a mantra. And ignore anything that BANGLES or WANGLES – they won't help at all.

BAIT HINT

If you want to trap a particular animal, break open its droppings to find out what it's been eating and bait the trap accordingly. Or, if you're not keen on rummaging in poo, use chocolate buttons.

Dont's...

... Bastard cashew nuts...
Bastard cashew nuts...

Cashew nuts are poisonous unless peeled and boiled and if you do boil them the fumes can blind you. So let's have a minute's silence for whoever found that out.

There you are Grandad, your Lupin tea

Lupins cause inflammation of the stomach and intestines that can prove fatal.

Buttercups cause severe inflammation of the intestines. I don't feel sorry for whoever found this out 'cos they are flowers and you're not meant to eat flowers.

Cowbane causes death within minutes. Ow!

Shark liver is poisonous. (It's all the neoprene from the wetsuits: they can't digest it.)

It's been 3 days now, it must be dead

Never pick up a snake until you are certain it is dead. Snakes feign death convincingly.
(Well, there's only one way to feign death.)

Wild potato fruits (which look like tomatoes) are poisonous. Wild tomato plants are edible but look like wild potatoes. So my advice is to get a couple of rocks and some earwigs and start grinding.

DON'T EAT WASPS!
They are the master-race and they don't like it.

Sigh.. Not tonight dear, I've a headache

TIME FOR A TREAT
Gather blackberries from brambles and then use the bramble canes to extract rabbits out of their sleeper holes. Sounds nasty but if you've been grinding earwigs all week...

Don't Hunt! It's illegal.

I hope this modest guide will encourage you to plunder meadow, hedgerow and fen till there is nothing left. Happy Foraging!

And remember – mangle, strangle, dangle, tangle, mangle, strangle, dangle, tangle, mangle, strangle, dangle!

ROWAN ATKINSON'S
FURNITURE MASTERCLASS

One of the maddening things about ready-assembled furniture is that it never comes with instructions. If you buy a new video camera or an iron or something and you can't get it to work, at least you can always blame the manual. But with furniture, it's always your responsibility.

Here's my essential guide to Getting It Right.

© Jim Marks Photography

Incorrect use of Planter

BASIC CHAIR TECHNIQUE

A chair is a very difficult object. LUDWIG MIES VAN DER ROHE

The domestic chair didn't become a common object until the 16th century. For thousands of years, only the powerful and important sat on them. Now, you too can learn to do it.

Good but feet should be a bit nearer the floor.

Bottom not near enough to chair.

Ideal if frightened of mice.

'The Sprinting Mantis' (advanced).

Commuter-style 'Reserved Seat' option.

Ideal if frightened of chairs.

Ideal if wet indoors.

No. (Newspaper is missing.)

CHAIR PLUS

You've now mastered single-chair operation. Let's move on. It's quite common to find several identical pieces of multiple-legged furniture clustered together. Powerful and important people use these for 'dinner parties' (long meals in the dark).

WRONG
Wine glass completely absent.

WRONG
Wine glass upside down.

WRONG
Wine glass too big.

BATHROOM FURNITURE

As a trained engineer, I tend to divide furniture into 'hardware', 'software' and 'wetware'. Hardware is stuff like tables, software is armchairs, beds and so forth. Wetware is my term for stools (also known as plop-plops) plus wee-wee and soaping the unmentionables.

English-style.

Scottish-style.

Couldn't get to the lavatory in time.

Not a shower (notice absence of soap-dish).

IMPORTANT! IT IS BAD MANNERS TO PUT YOUR FEET ON THE FURNITURE.

WRONG

Nearly right.

Nowhere near right.

Just plain silly.

51

FALCON VS FERRET

Which would you take home? Both are fearless, both are able to make a contribution to the family budget by bringing home a steady stream of furred and feathered game, both have been domesticated for millennia, but which one edges it for fun, form and function?

HERE'S HOW THEY SCORED ON OUR 10-POINT RATING SYSTEM.

TRAINABILITY: 9
You can get a falcon to perform to a very high standard by understanding its instincts. Training them is painstaking work and very rewarding but don't ever expect them to talk, or to hang upside down, or to adopt a baby rabbit.

THERAPEUTIC VALUE: 6
Watching a falcon fly, dive, swoop and strike is exhilarating, particularly if you've trained it yourself. But don't expect empathy or affection – their small reptilian brains don't have roon

ECONOMIC VALUE: 5
A well-trained falcon can be used to catch rabbits or quail but the hundreds of hours of training and supply of food probably mean you'll always be down on the deal in purely monetary terms.

EDIBILITY: 0
Even if you were desperate they're hardly worth the bother – their feathers weigh twice as much as their bones. Imagine the body of a thrush with huge talons and an abnormally large hooked beak – that's what a plucked falcon looks like.

CONTRIBUTIO TO THE LANGUAGE: 9
Few animals have contribute more: if you're 'fed up', 'at the end of your tether', 'in a bate', 'alluring' live in a 'mews act like a 'cad' go for an evening's 'boozing', you owe it all to falconry.*

DRESSING UP: 7
They look good in a hood, which can be quite flash and decked out with gaudy feathers and embroidery. And, at a pinch, their jesses (restraining straps) could be picked out in gold lamé. They look great on your arm at a party.

CUDDLEABILITY: 0
Falcons are magnificent and aloof. They're wonderful to look at, but remember you are only interesting to them as a source of food. So don't be surprised if they try to bite you.

FERTILITY: 2
You don't have to breed them, so unlikely to be an issue. If you do want 'baby falcons', get help, much as you would if you decided to keep pandas. It's about that easy.

BOTHER: 3
Lots of equipment, need for exercise, incompatability with other birds, risk of losing them altogether when they're flying. Difficulty in explaining 'accidents' to next-door neighbours' now hamsterless children.

SUPERPOWERS: 9
The peregrine falcon in a dive is the fastest animal on the planet reaching speeds of 215 mph (346 kph). A falcon's visual acuity is 8 times better than ours: they can spot a hamster from 2 miles/3.2 km away. As they dive, their eye muscles adjust the curvature of the eyeball to maintain sharp focus. When they hit, tendons in their claws snap shut to break their prey's neck (imagine being able to shatter a full wine bottle by squeezing your hand shut).

OVERALL SCORE: 52

CONTRIBUTION TO THE LANGUAGE: 2

Not much other than 'ferreting' in the sense of searching for something. Allegedly, 'ferret' comes from the Sanskrit root, 'bher-' meaning 'to carry or bear' from which we also get 'furtive', 'pheromone', 'fertile' and 'suffer'.

SUPERPOWERS: 7

One of the hardest bites in the animal kingdom, a ferret can snap a pencil without blinking and will crunch up every scrap of a bunny's bone, nail and fur for roughage. They can smell prey from hundreds of metres away, can drag a load 3 times their weight and leap 4 times their body length from a standing start. And they never get tired: they will kill rabbits non-stop, for as long as you let them.

THERAPEUTIC VALUE: 9

Ferrets are such cheerful, perky little animals they even get used as therapy animals for the severely depressed or trauma victims. They make very cute chirpy noises and do silly slightly unco-ordinated dances when you pay them attention. They aren't needy (like dogs), but are always pleased to see you (unlike cats).

TRAINABILITY: 6

You can teach a ferret to come to its name and roll over, but that's about it. They have absolutely no homing instinct and have a talent for getting themselves wedged in dark and difficult places. You don't really train them to catch rabbits – it's just what they do.

DRESSING UP: 7

There's quite a sub-culture of dressing up pet ferrets. 'Ferret World', the one-stop ferret shop, stock football strips, Hallowe'en and Father Christmas costumes, waxed jackets and a 'Phantom of the Opera' cape bought by ferret-owning barristers because it looks like a legal gown.

ECONOMIC VALUE: 9

A morning's ferreting can bring in a dozen or more rabbits: nutritious, delicious, free protein. To overcome any resistance from rabbit-lovers, mince the meat and make bunny burgers: much less squeam-inducing.

CUDDLEABILITY: 5

They look cute and will happily curl up in your lap and wriggle inside your jumper. But beware: their latin name, 'Mustela putorius furo', translates as 'musk-bearing, stinking thief' and it's not without cause. Ferrets stink. Be prepared to change clothes after handling (if it's a male, or hob, burning the clothes may be cheaper).

FERTILITY: 2

Slightly tricky – the jill (female) can die if they aren't mated when they're on heat, which is twice a year and a single jill could easily produce 27 kits a year. That's more than anyone needs. Try to borrow a vasectomised male (hoblet) but be warned: even safe ferret sex is rough, noisy and can go on for hours.

EDIBILITY: 0

Mustelids are edible, but it's hard to imagine a ferret fricassee (it's the smell). Besides, eating them is expressly forbidden in Leviticus 11:30: they are nailed as 'unclean' along with chameleons, lizards, snails and moles.

*'Bate' means pointless wing flapping. 'Booze' or 'bouse' is the term for the bird's drinking; a 'cadger' or 'cad' was the lowly person who carried the falcon for the falconer.

BOTHER: 8

No more work than a hamster – they sleep 18 hours a day. If you do take them out ferreting, all you'll need are 20 nets, a shovel (in case they fall asleep on the job) and the 'cojones' to knock a rabbit on the head.

OVERALL SCORE: 55

WHAT'S A FOOT?

FOOT: *the lower extremity of the leg below the ankle*

Feet excrete up to half a pint of moisture every day. They have over 250,000 sweat glands.

FOOT~SOLDIER

~HYPERHYDROSIS~ otherwise known as **SWEATY FEET**

BROMOHYDPOSIS IS THE MEDICAL TERM FOR FOOT ODOUR

THE *LARGEST* FEET IN THE WORLD BELONG TO ~*MATTHEW McGRORY* HIS FEET ARE A SIZE $28\frac{1}{2}$ US

£ **FOOTSIE** $

MADELINE ALBRECHT HOLDS THE WORLD RECORD FOR "MOST FEET SNIFFED" SHE WORKS FOR A RESEARCH COMPANY TESTING FOOT-CARE PRODUCTS FOR SCHOLL AND HAS SNIFFED APPROX-IMATELY 5,600 FEET.

barleycorn = $\frac{1}{3}$ of an inch

Feet size in England are measured in **BARLEYCORNS**

FOOTWORK

Your big toe is the most likely part of your body to be bitten by a vampire bat.

FOOTNOTE ~

PODOMANCY IS DIVINATION BY MEANS OF EXAMINING THE FEET

athlete's foot
in-growing toenail
love
death
health
wealth
miser
bunion
verruca

ELEPHANTS CAN LISTEN TO AND COMMUNICATE WITH EACH OTHER THROUGH THEIR FEET.

CAPTIVE ELEPHANTS CAN SUFFER BADLY FROM ATHLETE'S FOOT.

IN THAILAND IT IS EXTREMELY OFFENSIVE TO SHOW SOMEONE THE SOLE OF YOUR FOOT.

There is a significant correlation between foot-size and hand-size (but not between foot-size and penis size.)

—AS A CHILD, CHARLES DARWIN HAD PARTICULARLY SMELLY FEET—

FOOTSTOOL

8% OF AMERICANS ARE SO FRIGHTENED OF GERMS FROM LAVATORIES THAT THEY FLUSH THE LOO WITH THEIR FEET.

Charlie Chaplin's feet were insured for $150,000

Michael Flatley's were insured for $40,000,000

FOOTLIGHTS

INVITE A PIG TO YOUR TABLE AND HE'LL PUT HIS FEET ON IT.

Russian Proverb

A QUARTER OF THE BONES IN THE HUMAN BODY ARE IN THE FEET.

FOOT-FAULT

FI, FIE, FOE, FEMME! - *a foto luv story*

A wise man once said the reason men and women fight is that each assumes the other has their own characteristics. A wise woman immediately disagreed with him. 'Women are tough, unsentimental creatures,' she said, 'subduing horses with a glance and lifting molten metal with our bare hands, whereas men are simple and kind and enjoy cooking.' 'That's what I just said,' said the wise man under his breath. 'Don't you take that tone with me!!' screamed the wise woman, furiously packing her suitcase and folding some tea towels the while.

My point is this. Women think men know how to carve meat and that all they want is sex. But what men really yearn for is *love*, expressed in the form of pre-sliced hot food. Men think that if women ask a question they want to know the answer, when what they're really after is a long argument followed by chocolate. Try to see things *her way*. Walk a mile in her shoes (vacuuming and remembering birthdays as you go). Then complain that your feet hurt. That should do the trick…

So I set out to woo Ronni by turning up 45 minutes late…

…and then asking if she needed any light bulbs changed.

Soon, we were getting on like a house on fire. I made her laugh by regaling her with intimate descriptions of my girlfriend's accessories…

He's insane

Omg! Prada trainers!!

…then I asked her if she fancied something to eat.

This was a mistake, probably because she thought I was implying she was anorexic.

…so I hurriedly went off to take out the rubbish.

While I was away, I asked myself some pretty tough questions. Like, what's the difference between an elephant's bottom and a postbox.

When I returned, I tried to get back into Ronni's good books with a typically feminine non-sequitur. 'Fylfot!!' I exclaimed.

'What exactly do you mean by that?!?' she demanded icily.
'I'll show you, cow!' was my rejoinder.

'Fylfot' is the Old English word for a swastika, as I was able to demonstrate visually.

After beating my brains out, she seemed to relax a little.

'Come with me', she said, 'I've got something I think you'll find interesting.'

It was a portal into the underworld!!!

No, not really.
She wanted to show me her new belt.

We're happily married now, I'm pleased to say.

Though not to each other, thank God....

TO BE DISCONTINUED

57

FARSI PROVERBS

There are about 144 million speakers of Farsi (also known as Persian or Tajik) in the world. About half of them live in Iran, Afghanistan and Tajikstan where it is an official language. Persian is written in Arabic script, and Tajik in Cyrillic (Russian) script. In Afghanistan, Farsi is known as Dari. In some parts of Iran, Azerbaijan and Russia, it is known as Tat. This includes Christian-Tat and Judeo-Tat.

I Not everything that is round is a walnut.

II Not everything with a beard is your dad.

VIII For every grape there are a hundred wasps.

IX The bird in the air cannot be grilled.

X I used to feel sorry for myself because I had no shoes, until I met a man who was dead.

XVI Write kindness in marble and injuries in the dust.

XVII Wherever you go, the sky is the same colour.

XVIII Slanting baggage never reaches home.

III It is a mistake to point out the errors of elders.

IV The wise man sits on the hole in his carpet.

V He who wants a peacock must put up with India.

VI If my aunt had a beard, she would have been my uncle.

XIX Somersault in front of a buffoon!

XX A kind word can bring a snake out of a hole.

XXI If the sky falls, we shall all catch larks.

XI He who wears dark glasses, sees the world as dark.

XII Harvesting is not the work of a goat.

XIII A drowning man is not troubled by rain.

XIV He who has been bitten by a snake fears a piece of string.

VII Two watermelons cannot be carried in one hand.

XV Death is a camel that sleeps in everyone's house.

XXII The chicken has one leg.

FACRONYMS

by Craig Brown

FBI are detectives, searching for clues;
FTSE's your cue to switch off the news.
FIAT is the car giant once owned by Agnelli;
FFJ dress in tights and appear on the telly.
FCUK is for preppies who want to be Chav;
FAQ answers everything but the problem you have.
FOH is the theatre crush prior to the show;
FYI is a note sent by those in the know.
FDR (i) was the Pres behind the New Deal;
FDR (ii) is for spouses to holler and squeal.
FDR (iii) is a vestige that precedes a seizure;
FDR (iv) is the People's Democratic Front of Indonesia.
FDR (v) is the technical term for Black Box;
FLAK is the ultimate school of hard knocks.
FRL's famous tome is *The Common Pursuit*;
FO is for toffs who are awfully astute.
FYR means more work (and more waste of ink);
FT is a paper, pretty in pink.
FOE ride on boats, saving dolphins and whales
FBRs are no danger (except when one fails).
FSB's what the KGB calls itself now;
FIFA's perpetually caught up in a row.
FANY arrive at each battle wreck quick;
FIRST is Forschungs Institut fur Rechnerarchitektur und Software Technik.
FRSL is the authors you remember but dimly;
FAX is no acronym (it's short for facsimile).
FM or AM? It's always a wrench;
FFS is For Fuck's Sake (pardon my French).
FSA monitors those who beg, steal or borrow;
FSH is Full Service History (I'll read it tomorrow).
FOAF is geek-speak for Friend Of A Friend;
FIN is an airport in Papua New Guinea,
But also means Finnish, or Finis –

The End.

FTSE - *Financial Times* Stock Exchange; **FBI** - Federal Bureau of Investigation; **FIAT** - Fabbrica Italiana Automobili Torino; **FFJ** - Fathers For Justice; **FCUK** - French Connection UK; **FAQ** - Frequently Asked Questions; **FOH** - Front of House; **FYI** - For Your Information; **FDR (i)** - Franklin Delano Roosevelt; **FDR (ii)** Family Dispute Resolution; **FDR (iii)** Firearm Discharge Residue; **FDR (iv)** Front Democrasi Rakjat; **FDR (v)** Flight Data Recorder; **FLAK** - FlugAbwehrKanone (German for Anti-Aircraft Guns); **FRL** - Professor F. R. (Frank Raymond) Leavis; **FO** - Foreign Office; **FYR** - For Your Reference; **FT** - *Financial Times*; **FOE** - Friends of the Earth; **FBR** - Fast Breeder Reactor; **FSB** - Federainaya Sluzhba Bezopasnosti; **FIFA** - Fédération Internationale de Football Association; **FANY** - First Aid Nursing Yeomanry; **FRSL** - Fellow of the Royal Society of Literature; **FM** - Frequency Modulation; **FSA** - Financial Services Authority; **FIN** - Three-letter shortcode for Finschhafen Airport, Papua New Guinea.

Grim Fairy Tales

Little Red Riding Hood

In 1697, a French poet named Charles Perrault (1628-1703) published eight traditional oral tales for the first time. In his version of Little Red Riding Hood, 'Le Petit Chaperon Rouge', the wolf (dressed as the Grandma he has just eaten) is a werewolf. To distract him and play for time, Red Riding Hood performs a full striptease, taking off one article of clothing at a time until she is stark naked and the werewolf is mad with lust. When he begs her to come to bed with him, she makes the excuse that she needs a pee. 'Do it in the bed,' gabbles the desperate werewolf, but the girl goes outside and escapes.

My what a big willy you have, Grandma!

DA DA!

Sleeping Beauty

In Giambattista Basile's bracingly titled 1634 collection, 'Lo cunto de li cunti' (that's 'The Tale of Tales' in Neapolitan, of course), a piece of flax gets under Sleeping Beauty's fingernail, which sends her to sleep. A foreign king stumbles upon her and finds her so irresistible he ravishes her, despite her death-like slumber. (Oh, perlease, what has monarchy sunk to!) Nine months later she gives birth to twins – while still asleep – and only wakes up when one of these, while searching for a nipple, sucks on her finger and removes the bewitching flax.

You came back...

Cinderella

In the 7th edition of the Grimm Brothers' collection (1857), Cinderella's step-sisters are as evil as we have come to expect them to be, but they are also beautiful – a chilling touch. Their mother, equally beautiful and a psychopathic sadist to boot, presents them with a knife and tells them to cut their feet down to size until the golden slipper fits. 'When you are queen you will no longer have to go on foot,' is her icy rationale. The mutilated feet are only discovered when a pigeon sees blood pouring out of the slippers. The sisters hobble along to Cinderella's wedding anyway, but the pigeons are on hand to peck their eyes out.

Off with her feet!

Many fairy stories started as traditional tales told by adults, to adults. They were passed on, spoken aloud, for hundreds of years before they were ever written down. Here are some early versions of familiar scenes from what have since become best-loved children's classics

Pinocchio

In Carlo Collodi's original story, first published in 1883, Pinocchio falls asleep in front of the fire and his feet burn off. (By this point he's already murdered the talking insect that will one day become known as Jiminy Cricket with a wooden mallet.) Later, a cat and a fox hang Pinocchio by the neck from an oak tree and wait for him to die. He then gets turned into a donkey, tied to a rock and thrown over a cliff. This is because the man who bought him wants to kill and skin him in order to make a drum.

'ev you gotta light boy?

Snow White

In the Grimm Brothers' version of 1812, the huntsman is sent by Snow White's jealous real mother (not her step-mother) to bring back her daughter's lungs and liver, which she plans to salt, cook and eat. (In earlier variants of the tale, she also asks for a phial of the girl's blood to drink, helpfully suggesting that the murderer uses her severed toe as a stopper.) The queen gets her come-uppance when she is forced to attend Snow White's wedding wearing red-hot iron shoes and dance in them until she drops down dead.

Hmmm, pleasant little vintage!

The Frog Prince

One of the oldest-known versions of the story is a folktale from Hungary. The frog is guarding a well and won't allow the girl to draw water for her family. His suggestions become ever more bold until finally he demands that the girl's father let him go to bed with her. The thirsty father agrees and next morning the family find a handsome young man lying in her arms. Just to remove any doubts over what has happened, the tale ends: 'they hastened to celebrate the wedding, so that the christening might not follow it too soon.'

... but this is a Grimm Fairy Tale, my dear -
you'll have to go a lot further than that...

Finger Games

How to win at
Rock-Paper-Scissors*

The oldest game

Recent research into the human brain has revealed that the same area that controls our tongues and larynx also controls the movement of our hands and fingers. Some even think we used our hands to talk before our voices. So humans may have been playing RPS even longer than we've been talking (replace scissors with knives and paper with leaves and a Neanderthal version is perfectly possible). After all, it is a universal way of solving problems, is played everywhere and requires no board or fancy equipment.

Pure luck

Most beginners make the fatal error of believing RPS is a game governed by the laws of chance. In fact it is as psychologically charged and complex as chess. It even has its own international regulatory body, The World RPS Society based in Toronto, who mount annual world championships.

RPS Tactics

Here's our cut-out-and-keep guide to winning the oldest game of all.

Stage 1: Beginners

There are two fundamental RPS maxims:

MAXIM 1: Rock is for rookies

Never play rock as your first move.
As the old adage goes, 'rock is for rookies.'

The best move is to play paper, but most people can work this out, so play scissors.

However, due to this fact appearing in pieces like this; the top strategy is now to play rock.

MAXIM 2: Know your opponent

If your opponent appears aggressive they are most likely to play rock.
Action: Play paper.

If your opponent appears thoughtful, they are most likely to play paper.
Action: Play scissors.

If your opponent seems cocky or devious, they will probably play scissors.
Action: Play rock.

Stage 2: Intermediate

In best-of-three play, there are a number of combinations that will keep your opponent guessing.

The Avalanche

Rock-Rock-Rock – ultra-offensive strategy that works because after a single aggressive throw most opponents assume you would be reckless to throw a second, and a complete nutter to throw a third.

The Bureaucrat

Paper-Paper-Paper – the ultimate softly-softly strategy. This works particularly well against rock-throwing show-offs with a serious avalanche habit. Also, the risk of coming up against scissors is lower: it's easily the least popular throw, only played 29.6% of the time.

The Toolbox

Scissors-Scissors-Scissors – not to be used against beginners (owing to their fondness for rock) but can be particularly effective if you 'spring-load', i.e. push your scissor fingers against the inside of your hand so that they get fired out quickly when throwing.

The Crescendo

Paper-Scissors-Rock – this gambit gives the illusion of weakness with its opening throw but ends in a devastating rock climax which will shatter your opponent's confidence.

Fistful of Dollars

Rock-Paper-Paper – the swift switch from offence to defence will unnerve even the best opponent. Most effective against a player who is trying to control his/her temper.

Stage 3: Advanced

Tells

All but the most professional RPS players reveal tiny changes to their behaviour or expressions that help give away their next move. Inexperienced players tend to change their stance as they change their throw and stay in the same position if they plan to repeat the previous throw.

Here are some useful pointers.

Jaw-clench – adrenalin causes people to clench their jaws to better absorb a punch in the face. A jaw-clencher will always throw rock.

Little finger knuckle – if the knuckle of your opponent's little finger moves slightly inwards, this means he or she is about to extend his/her ring and index fingers into a scissors. You can also tell a lot about a player by the angle of their scissors.

Curve-ball – in professional play, a paper-throw must have the palm parallel to the ground, to avoid confusion with scissors. As a result, players often slightly curl their forearm towards their face when playing this move.

Professionalism and borderline cheating

Cloaking – making it look like you are throwing one move before switching at the last moment to another. Be careful: push this too far and the referee will award the game to your opponent.

Throw counting – paying careful attention to your opponent's throws to find a pattern. Humans are driven by patterns. This can be difficult, especially if your opponent clocks that you are a counter, and responds with lively, off-putting banter.

Crystal ball – this technique requires the gift of the gab – pretend to predict your opponent's next move – 'You're going to choose scissors again' – to narrow his/her options.

Overwhelming your opponent – if you have a physical advantage, try flexing your muscles, grunting and generally acting like a testosterone-fuelled Neanderthal before playing an unexpected scissors.

RPS: THE FACTS

The modern version of RPS is a Far Eastern game originally played during Chinese New Year.

When it first arrived in Japan in the late 19th century it was an adult drinking game played in the bars of Tokyo's red-light district.

In 2005 Christie's won a $20 million contract to sell a corporate client's collection of Picassos and Van Goghs after a game of rock, paper, scissors.

The elements alter from country to country: in France it's 'Rock-Scissors-Well'; in Malaysia, 'Rock-Beak-Well' and in Vietnam, 'Elephant-Human-Ant.'

The apology – making your throw extremely late and responding to the inevitable complaint with: 'Sorry, my fault. Let's do it again.' Reverse psychology dictates he or she will almost always attempt the same throw again. Use this gambit sparingly – some referees consider it cheating.

Further reading

The RPS bible is *The Official Rock Paper Scissors Strategy Guide* by Douglas & Graham Walker (Simon & Schuster, 2004) or you could visit their website: www.worldrps.com

* still called 'Scissors-Paper-Stone' by older British players.

RPS INTERNATIONAL

Jenken or Jan Ken Pon (Japan)
Kai bai bo (Korea)
Janjii (Thailand)
Roshambo (Southwestern USA)
Shnik Shnak Shnuk (Germany)
Farggling (USA)
Ching Chong Chow
(South Africa)

'My mum told me, "don't throw stones, don't play with scissors," I bet you're choking on those words now, eh mum?'

- Dave Bradbury, 1943 UK RPS champion.

Infundibuliform

Toroid

Please take a few moments to answer the following short questionnaire.

1. How many times have you been lost for words when trying to describe the shape of something?

a) Literally millions of times, it drives me mad!!
b) Fairly often, it bothers me quite a lot.

c) Relatively rarely, I am rather articulate.
d) Who are you? How did you get this number?

That's it. Well done. If you answered a, b or c, score two points - your worries are over. By memorising the list of *form*-type words on these pages, you will soon be *'top* of the form' and get to Cambridge University with the chance to become the next Stephen Hawking, Stephen Fry or Stephen Poliakoff. Pretty well everyone at Cambridge called Stephen becomes world-famous and nearly all of them managed it simply because they understood correct *form*. Don't worry if you're not called Stephen *at the moment*, your tutor or spymaster can help you fill in The Form in due course.

If you answered d, you may be interested to know that you are suffering from Rajasthani Call-Centre Syndrome, where you imagine that you are hearing voices in your telephone with impenetrable sub-continental accents asking for the second digit of your security code. Regrettably, this condition is incurable, but can be relieved by being incomprehensible back. Pepper your responses generously with some of the words here and just hear those voices ring off in despair!

Acorn-shaped: Balanoid

Apple-shaped: Pomiform

Arrow-shaped: Beloid; sagittal

Awl-shaped: Subulate

Axe-shaped: Securiform

Barrel-shaped: Dolioform

Basin-shaped: Pelviform

Bell-shaped: Campanulate

Berry-shaped: Aciniform

Boat-shaped: Cymbiform; navicular; scaphoid

Boil-shaped: Bulliform

Bonnet-shaped: Mitrate

Book-shaped: Libriform

Bristle-shaped: Setiform

Brush-shaped: Aspergilliform; muscariform

Bunch-of-grapes-shaped: Uvelloid

Buttock-shaped: Natiform

Cake-shaped: Placentiform

Cap-shaped: Pileated

Caterpillar-shaped: Eruciform

Chisel-shaped: Scalpriform

Claw-shaped: Unguiform

Cloud-shaped: Nubiform

Coin-shaped: Nummiform

Comb-shaped: Pectiniform; cteniform

Cone-shaped: Infundibuliform

Cow-shaped: Boviform

Crescent-shaped: Lunate; menisciform

Cucumber-shaped: Cucumiform

Cup-shaped: Poculiform; scyphiform

Cushion-shaped: Pulvilliform

Dagger-shaped: Pugioniform

Dart-shaped: Belemnoid

Doughnut-shaped: Toroid

Drop-shaped: Guttiform

Drum-shaped: Tympaniform

Ear-shaped: Auriform

Egg-shaped: Ooidal

Fan-shaped: Rhipidate; flabelliform

Feather-shaped: Pinnate

Flowerpot-shaped: Vasculiform

Fork-shaped: Furcular

Fringe-shaped: Laciniform

Frog-shaped: Raniform

Funnel-shaped: Chaonoid

Girdle-shaped: Zosteriform

Goat-shaped: Capriform

Groove-shaped: Sulciform

Half-moon-shaped: Semilunate

Hammer-shaped: Malleiform

Handle-shaped: Manubrial

Hatchet-shaped: Pelecoidal

Helmet-shaped: Cassideous; galeated

Herring-shaped: Harengiform

Hood-shaped: Cuculate

Hook-shaped: Unciform

Horn-shaped: Corniculate; corniform; ceratoid

Horseshoe-shaped: Hippocrepian

Ivy-shaped: Hederiform

Jellyfish-shaped: Medusiform

Jug-shaped: Urceolate

Keyhole-shaped: Clithridiate

Kidney-shaped: Nephroid; reniform

Knife-shaped: Cultriform

Ladder-shaped: Scalariform

Leaf-shaped: Phylliform; foliform

Mosquito-shaped: Culciform

Mouse-shaped: Muriform

Mulberry-shaped: Moriform

Needle-shaped: Acicular

Net-shaped: Clathrate

Nipple-shaped: Mamilliform

Nose-shaped: Nasutiform

Nostril-shaped: Nariform

Nut-shaped: Nuciform

Oar-shaped: Remiform

Oat-shaped: Aveniform

Oval-shaped: Vulviform

Owl-shaped: Strigiform

Oyster-shaped: Ostreiform

Paintbrush-shaped: Pencilliform

Palm-leaf-shaped: Spadicious

Partition-shaped: Septiform

Pea-shaped: Pisiform

Pebble-shaped: Calciform

Pincer-shaped: Cheliform

Pine-cone-shaped: Pineal

Pipe-shaped: Fistuliform

Plate-shaped: Lamelliform

Pouch-shaped: Scrotiform

Purse-shaped: Bursiform

Ribbon-shaped: Taenioid

Rice-shaped: Riziform

Ring-shaped: Cingular; circinate; cricoid

Rod-shaped: Vergiform

Rodent-shaped: Gliriform

Roof-shaped: Tectiform

S-shaped: Annodated

Saddle-shaped: Selliform

Saucer-shaped: Acetabuliform

Sausage-shaped: Allantoid

Saw-shaped: Serriform

Scimitar-shaped: Acinaciform

Screw-shaped: Helicoid

Seaweed-shaped: Fucoid

Shark-shaped: Squaliform

Shield-shaped: Aspidate; peltastiform; scutiform

Sheep-shaped: Oviform

Sickle-shaped: Drepaniform

Sieve-shaped: Coliform

Slipper-shaped: Soleiform

Slug-shaped: Limaciform

Socket-shaped: Glenoid

Spade-shaped: Palaceous

Spinning-top-shaped: Trochiform

Spur-shaped: Calcariform

Stirrup-shaped: Stapediform

Sword-shaped: Xiphoid

Tail-shaped: Caudiform

Tear-shaped: Lachrymiform

Thorn-shaped: Spiniform; aculeiform

Toad-shaped: Bufoniform

Tongue-shaped: Linguiform

Tower-shaped: Pygoidal; turriform

Tree-shaped: Arborescent; dendriform

Trumpet-shaped: Buccinal

Turnip-shaped: Napiform

U-shaped: Hyoid

Umbrella-shaped: Umbraculiform; pileiform

Violin-shaped: Panduriform

Wedge-shaped: Sphenoid; cuneiform

Whip-shaped: Flagelliform

Wolf-shaped: Lupiform

Woodpecker-shaped: Piciform

Worm-shaped: Vermiform

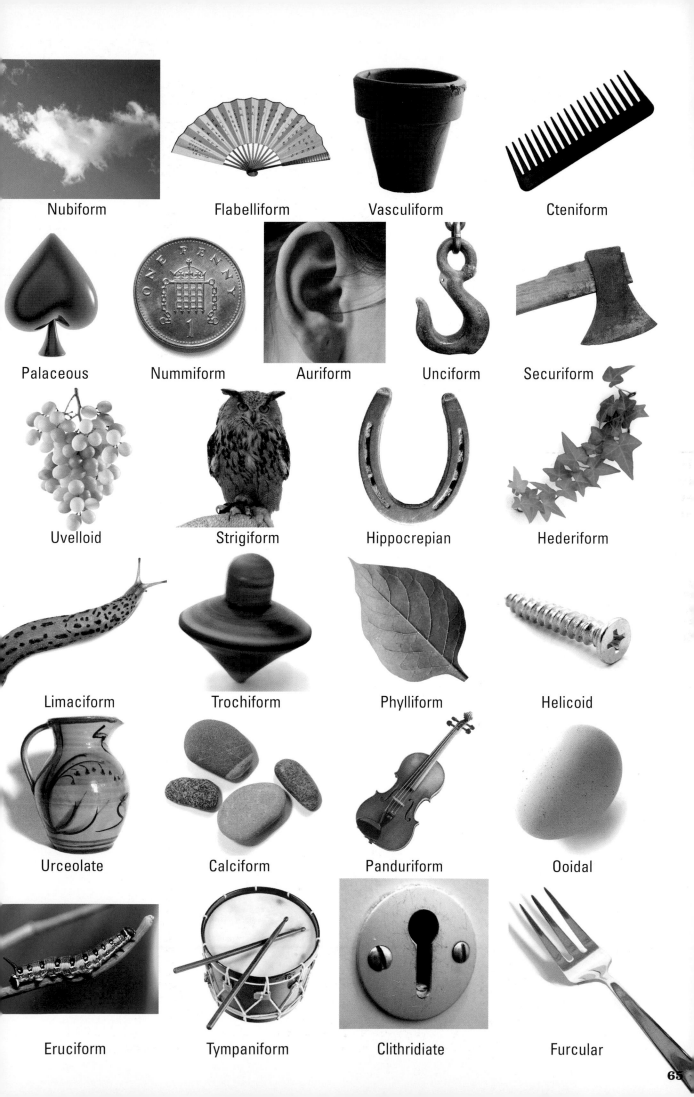

Nubiform

Flabelliform

Vasculiform

Cteniform

Palaceous

Nummiform

Auriform

Unciform

Securiform

Uvelloid

Strigiform

Hippocrepian

Hederiform

Limaciform

Trochiform

Phylliform

Helicoid

Urceolate

Calciform

Panduriform

Ooidal

Eruciform

Tympaniform

Clithridiate

Furcular

FOOTBALL
IN MOUTH

Think of a number between 10 and 11.
RON ATKINSON

Argentina are the second best team in the world and there is no higher praise than that. **KEVIN KEEGAN**

Chile have three options - they could win or they could lose. **KEVIN KEEGAN**

When England go to Turkey there could be fatalities - or even worse, injuries.
PHIL NEAL

I'd like to play for an Italian club, like Barcelona.
MARK DRAPER

I can see the carrot at the end of the tunnel. **STUART PEARCE**

It all went a bit grape-shaped. **JASON McATEER**

I always used to put my right boot on first, and then obviously my right sock. **BARRY VENISON**

I'd love to be a mole on the wall in the Liverpool dressing room at half time. **KEVIN KEEGAN**

Don't ask me what a typical Brazilian is because I don't know what a typical Brazilian is. But Romario was a typical Brazilian.
BOBBY ROBSON

If you can't stand the heat in the dressing room, get out of the kitchen. **TERRY VENABLES**

Goalkeepers aren't born today until they're in their late twenties or thirties. **KEVIN KEEGAN**

The Germans only have one player under 22, and he's 23.
KEVIN KEEGAN

People will look at Bowyer and Woodgate and say, 'Well, there's no mud without flames'. **GORDON TAYLOR**

Unfortunately, we keep kicking ourselves in the foot.
RAY WILKINS

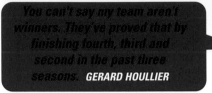

You can't say my team aren't winners. They've proved that by finishing fourth, third and second in the past three seasons. **GERARD HOULLIER**

Well, Clive, it's all about the two Ms - movement and positioning. **RON ATKINSON**

And Seaman, just like a falling oak, manages to change direction. **JOHN MOTSON**

The tide is very much in our court now. **KEVIN KEEGAN**

We must have had 99% of the match. It was the other 3% that cost us. **RUUD GULLIT**

That could have been his second yellow card - if he'd already got his first one of course. **TREVOR BROOKING**

I was feeling as sick as the proverbial donkey. **MICK McCARTHY**

We don't want our players to be monks. We want them to be better football players because a monk doesn't play football at this level. **BOBBY ROBSON**

Viv Anderson has pissed a fatness test. **JOHN HELM**

At this level, if five or six players don't turn up, you'll get beat. **KEVIN KEEGAN**

You're on your own out there with ten mates.
MICHAEL OWEN

He may well yet pull his team from the edge of the cliff by the scruff of its neck into the land of milk and honey.
JONATHAN HAYWARD

He dribbles a lot and the opposition don't like it - you can see it all over their faces. **RON ATKINSON**

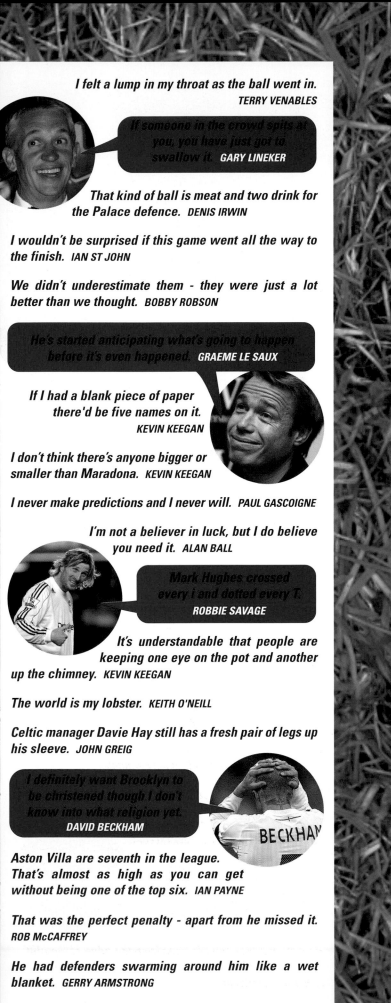

I felt a lump in my throat as the ball went in.
TERRY VENABLES

If someone in the crowd spits at you, you have just got to swallow it. **GARY LINEKER**

That kind of ball is meat and two drink for the Palace defence. **DENIS IRWIN**

I wouldn't be surprised if this game went all the way to the finish. **IAN ST JOHN**

We didn't underestimate them - they were just a lot better than we thought. **BOBBY ROBSON**

He's started anticipating what's going to happen before it's even happened. **GRAEME LE SAUX**

If I had a blank piece of paper there'd be five names on it. **KEVIN KEEGAN**

I don't think there's anyone bigger or smaller than Maradona. **KEVIN KEEGAN**

I never make predictions and I never will. **PAUL GASCOIGNE**

I'm not a believer in luck, but I do believe you need it. **ALAN BALL**

Mark Hughes crossed every i and dotted every T. **ROBBIE SAVAGE**

It's understandable that people are keeping one eye on the pot and another up the chimney. **KEVIN KEEGAN**

The world is my lobster. **KEITH O'NEILL**

Celtic manager Davie Hay still has a fresh pair of legs up his sleeve. **JOHN GREIG**

I definitely want Brooklyn to be christened though I don't know into what religion yet. **DAVID BECKHAM**

Aston Villa are seventh in the league. That's almost as high as you can get without being one of the top six. **IAN PAYNE**

That was the perfect penalty - apart from he missed it. **ROB McCAFFREY**

He had defenders swarming around him like a wet blanket. **GERRY ARMSTRONG**

I just wonder what would have happened if the shirt had been on the other foot. **MIKE WALKER**

For thousands of years China had a tradition of witty and influential court jesters with fantastic names. Their skill in using humour to escape punishment or gently ridicule their employers seems peculiarly modern. Which one are you?

BALDY CHUNYU

King Weiwang, ruler of the state of Qi from 378 to 343 BC was rescued from a life of drink and womanising by his fool Baldy Chunyu who told him a riddle in which the King was portrayed as a rather ineffective large bird squatting on the palace roof.

TWISTY POLE

The feckless emperor Qin Er Shi (229-207 BC) decided he wanted to lacquer the Great Wall. The famous fool and dwarf Twisty Pole subverted this lunacy by declaring it a brilliant plan but wondered how practical it would be to build a drying room large enough for the lacquer to harden.

NEWLY POLISHED MIRROR

The Emperor Zhuangzong (ruled 923-926) had a particularly feisty fool called Newly Polished Mirror who was once bold enough to strike the emperor's face, plunging the court into shock. Luckily, the emperor saw the funny side and rewarded him generously.

IN FULL STREAMER

A fool who was kidnapped by rebels during the reign of Emperor Xuanzong (685-762) and kept himself alive by entertaining his captors. He later managed to persuade the emperor of his loyalty by recounting dreams he'd had which showed the rebellion would fail and he would be released.

FITTING NEW BRIDLE

When threatened by a thuggish governor (who had recently burnt a rival city to the ground), he saved

68

CHINESE FOOL AM I?

You are definitely NOT an ancient Chinese fool. — NO →

Do you hate your boss?

NO →

YES →

Do you resent paying your taxes?

Are you popular at parties?

NO

NO

NO

Are you a fan of the outdoors?

YES

Do you prefer A Question of Sport to The Apprentice?

NO

YES

Do you think you have psychic powers?

YES

YES

NO

YES

· YOU ARE ·
· NOT A CHINESE FOOL ·

· YOU ARE ·
· TRULY ASSISTING UPRIGHTNESS ·
TAX TO PAY

· YOU ARE ·
FITTING NEW BRIDLE ·

YOU ARE
SCORCHING VIRTUE

· YOU ARE ·
· IN FULL STREAMER ·

himself through the speed of his wit. When asked if he would beg for mercy, he said he had no need to beg as he could live by selling the charcoal produced by the governor's pyromania.

TRULY ASSISTING UPRIGHTNESS
Chinese fools often pushed it too far. This one was executed by Emperor Dezong (742-805) for satirising tax policies by dressing as a pauper. This was an unpopular decision: most people felt strongly it was the place of jesters to 'provide indirect advice' through humour.

SCORCHING VIRTUE
Scorching Virtue was severely punished for criticising the prime minister of the Emperor Huizong (1082-1135) who had flattened a village to build a new park. Wittily comparing it to another park which looked like a bank of clouds, the new park, he said, was like a downpour, because it had caused so many tears to fall.

GRADUALLY STRETCHING TALLER
Gradually Stretching Taller persuaded Emperor Liezu (d 949) to stop overtaxing his subjects by suggesting that even the rain was refusing to enter the city for fear of being taxed. The emperor laughed, repealed the offending law and the heavens immediately opened.

WILD PIG
Emperor Xizong (1119-1149) fancied himself as a great footballer. 'If I sat an exam in dribbling, I'd come top of the class' he told his fool, Wild Pig. 'Yes, but you'd end up at the bottom of the league of good rulers,' came the quick retort. The Emperor laughed and gave up his dreams of football glory.

Jimmy Carr's Famous Fannies

TINKLING FANNY

Fanny Mendelssohn was the older sister of the composer Felix. The more famous male Mendelssohn readily admitted that she was a better pianist than he was, but due to 19th-century attitudes towards women, she never reached the fame that her talent deserved. Fanny composed 466 pieces of music, several of which were published under Felix's name. Queen Victoria's favourite Mendelssohn song was 'Italien' from his Op. 8 collection: it was actually written by Fanny. Fanny's father is reported as telling her: 'For you music can and must only be an ornament. You must prepare more earnestly and eagerly for your real calling, I mean the state of a housewife.' Fanny and Felix both died of a stroke in the same year, 1847. She was 41; he was 37.

FLYING FANNY

Francina 'Fanny' Blankers-Koen was a 30-year-old Dutch athlete and mother of two known as 'Amazing Fanny' or 'The Flying Housewife'. At the 1948 London Olympics, she won 4 gold medals, trouncing the entire British Olympic team single-handed – Britain only won 3 golds that year – and remains one of just four people (and the only woman) to win 4 track and field golds at a single Games. During her career, she set world records in 7 different events. In 1999, the IAAF voted her 'Female Athlete of the Century'.

ROCKY FANNY

Fanny is a minor planet orbiting the sun, otherwise known as Asteroid 821. Discovered in 1916 by German astronomer Max Wolf (1863-1932), nobody knows why he chose that name. Wolf, a pioneer of astrophotography, also discovered 247 other asteroids, including the equally mysteriously named 456 Abnoba, 810 Atossa, 866 Fatme, 868 Lova, 1661 Granule, 449 Hamburga and 1703 Barry.

BRAWNY FANNY

Fanny Brawn was the love of the poet John Keats's life. Only 1.5 m (5 ft) tall and generally uncomfortable in the company of women, Keats's letters to Fanny are classics in the art of love letters, and the two secretly became engaged before the affair was brought to an end by Keats's untimely death from tuberculosis at the age of 25. Fanny later married and had 3 children but never took off the ring given to her by Keats, and never told her husband about her former love.

FUSSY FANNY

Fanny Owen was a close friend of Charles Darwin's sisters and became his girlfriend while he was at Cambridge. He used to go riding with her, they played billiards together and he taught her how to shoot pheasants. She ended the relationship early in 1930, because Darwin preferred to spend the Christmas holidays organising his beetle collection rather than staying with his potential in-laws.

PRAWNY FANNY

Pioneering 60s TV chef Fanny Cradock was abandoned by her mother Bijou on her grandmother's billiard table at the age of one and was bought up by her grandparents for the next 9 years. She was married 4 times (twice bigamously), and believed that she was psychic, getting expelled from boarding school for holding a séance in the library. This Fanny is credited with inventing the prawn cocktail.

PRETTY FANNY

Former Prime Minister Arthur Balfour (1848-1930) was nicknamed 'Pretty Fanny' at Eton and Cambridge due to his lovely manners and the great importance he paid to appearance. Nephew to former Prime Minister Robert Gascoyne-Cecil, 3rd Marquis of Salisbury, he got his big break in politics when his uncle made him Minister for Ireland.
It was this act of nepotism that led to the phrase 'bob's your uncle'. Balfour was also nicknamed 'Clara', 'Niminy-Pimminy' and Lisping Hawthorn Bird'. He never married.

TINNED FANNY

Fanny Adams was originally the name given by British sailors to tinned meat (especially mutton) and the stew or hash made from it, first recorded in print in a dictionary of slang in 1889. The origin of the term is grisly and relates to the famous murder of an 8-year old girl in Alton, Hampshire in 1867. The murderer, a solicitor's clerk named Frederick Baker, was hanged in front of 5,000 people at Winchester later that year. In 1869, the Royal Navy introduced a new 'convenience food' mutton ration. This looked so unpleasant that sailors compared it, with macabre humour, to the horribly dismembered remains of 'Sweet Fanny Adams'. Sailors adapted the large packing cans in which the tinned meat arrived for use as impromptu mess tins, and, in today's Navy, mess tins in general are still referred to as 'fannies'. The expression 'sweet FA' (meaning 'nothing') and used as a euphemism for 'F*** All', derives from the coincidental similarity of the letters FA.

KISSY FANNY

One tradition in the French game of pétanque, or *boules*, is that when a player fails to score a single point, he must kiss the bottom of a girl called Fanny. At many pétanque courts, you can see a bare-bottomed statue or picture of 'Fanny', in case there is no obliging young lady of that name available. Legend has it that the original Fanny was a waitress from the Savoie region of France who, just after the First World War, offered the local mayor a kiss on her nether regions as a consolation prize for coming last. You can purchase your very own fanny here: www.laboulebleue.fr/en/Catalogue/Boutique.htm

NAUGHTY FANNY

Fanny Hill is considered to be the first modern erotic novel. It was written in 1748 by John Cleland and was originally called *Memoirs of a Woman of Pleasure*. Many believe that this is where the rude sense of the word 'fanny' comes from. It caused a scandal at the time, and despite his careful use of euphemisms (the male member is referred to by 50 different names) Cleland was imprisoned briefly and the Bishop of London blamed the book for causing 2 small earthquakes.

Fantastic Flushers

Underwatercloset

with
Sir John Flushing
and Dr Lulu Ubenda

by Ted Dewan

This WWII submarine toilet (or "head") was shared by 20 men. The queues for the heads were long because they were so complicated to flush.

Bombs Away!

Submarine toilets had to flush waste into the sea at high pressure (30 - 100 psi). To achieve this, a reservoir tank was connected up to the main compressed-air line. The reservoir pressure had to be high enough to overcome sea pressure. Before flushing, it was essential to ensure the discharge-to-sea valve was fully open. Levers which controlled the flushing system and positioned a non-return flap had to be manipulated in a strict operational sequence.

SPLOOFSH!

Turn red valve above the toilet to fill the bowl with water halfway

Flushing the toilet was nearly as lethal as launching the other sort of "torpedoes". If a sailor got it wrong, it could result in painfully high-pressure sewage blasting out the toilet back in the sub. This was known as "getting your own back".

Nazi Poop Deck

The toilet on the German WWII U-boat submarine *U-1206* proved to be too much for one Captain Schlitt who made an error when flushing the toilet during a drill. Captain Schlitt's fumbled flush forced gushes of seawater into the sub which leaked down into the battery compartment. The sub then had to rise to the surface to ventilate the toxic chlorine gas given off by the water-logged batteries. Once on the surface, the *U-1206* was spotted by an RAF aircraft and depth-charged, sinking the entire ship.

When finished, lift and lower this lever to flush, but only after reservoir pressure is high enough to discharge waste, and a non-return flap is engaged

The Toilets of the WWII Submarine USS Pampanito

TARGET PRACTICE

Men and boys seem to have difficulties aiming their pee due to a combination of inattention, carelessness, and unexpected diversions of the urine stream caused by the occasional partial obstruction in the nozzle of the penis. Since it seems that the guys never learn to take preventative action, here are several solutions to the undesired effects of this age-old problem and the related disharmony between the sexes.

The Ups and Downs of Toilet Sharing

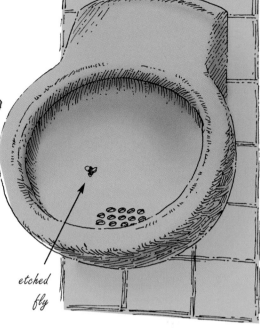

etched fly

Women complain about men failing to lift the seat and peeing all over it. A Japanese design solves the problem by featuring a seat that lifts itself into an upright position.

But women also complain to men for leaving the seat up when they've finished urinating. The gracious thing for men to do is lift the seat, urinate, and then return the seat to its down position for the next female user.

Aiming to Keep the WC Clean

Inspired by a Victorian innovation that first appeared in London, these modern urinals in Amsterdam have a picture of a fly etched into the porcelain. If a guy sees a fly in a urinal, he aims at it. And because the guy is thinking and aiming at the fly, the mens' room stays five times cleaner than it would without the fly because there's less urine spraying in an unruly fashion. By the end of the session, it becomes apparent that the fly is a fake. But such is the joy of the ingeniousness of this idea, it is likely that 'aim for the fly' might become incorporated into a repeat user's private peeing ritual.

If this sounds like too much work for the lads, the celebrated mathematician John Banderob once put it in precise mathematical language, *"a woman's need to have the seat down is greater than a man's need to leave it up."*

Uro-Cup

This urinal employs a device for improving aim by once again appealing to male instincts. The toy plastic football goal has a ball hanging from the top which changes colour when soaked in urine. However, this solution is not a serious attempt to keep public mens' rooms cleaner, because the goalposts deviate the streams of urine somewhat haphazardly.

NOW WASH YOUR HANDS

Fried Fish

Butter Hamlets are small, brightly coloured tropical fish which live in the western Atlantic. They come in 10 different colours – this one was a lovely purplish hue. Butter hamlets make distinctive low-frequency mating calls that are too deep to be heard with the human ear, which scientists believe may prove they are actually 10 different species. They are hermaphrodites that carry both ripe eggs and fertile sperm and mate by intertwining, so that the hamletty part goes in the buttery bit and vice versa. Try not to think about it.

The **Death Valley Pupfish** (*Cyrinodon salinus salinus*) is the last known species of fish still living in Death Valley, California, in a creek called Salt Creek that used to be a lake called 'Lake Manly'. The entire world's population lives within a half-mile radius of each other. Also called the Salt Creek Pupfish, the salty nature of its habitat means seasoning is unnecessary. Not to be confused with the Devil's Hole Pupfish, found only in a single desert spring in Nevada. Or with what's in the picture, which, of course, is haddock.

Humuhumunukunukuapua'a (*Rhinecanthus rectangulus*) as shown here is the state fish of Hawaii. Its name means 'triggerfish with a snout like a pig' and it is also known as the Picasso Triggerfish, although its wildly glowing patterns make it look more like a Mondrian or an African national flag. It has blue teeth. It's not the longest name for a fish in Hawaiian: that belongs to the *lauwiliwilinukunuku'oi'oi* ('long-snouted fish shaped like a wiliwili'). A *humuhumunukunukuapua'a* can change colour startlingly if threatened, but is drab if asleep or in fishcake mode.

The male **Sunset Gourami** (*Colisa lalia*) is one of the most beautiful and distinctive of aquarium fish. It is a metallic pale blue, with bright red vertical stripes. The females are not nearly as attractive as the males, being a plain grey with the faintest trace of stripes. We chose to fry a male one, for obvious reasons. An alternative might have been a 'balloon pink' kissing gourami – or possibly a green one. But, though these have luscious-looking lips, the effect is rather spoiled by them being lined with horny teeth.

Siamese Fighting Fish (*Betta splendens*) are used to being battered. They are bred in Thailand especially to fight, and, before being popped into hot oil, are kept in jam-jars out of sight of other fish, as they can try to swim through the glass to get at a potential opponent and injure themselves. Though ordinary looking and dull green or brown in their natural habitat, selective breeding has produced varieties with spectacular colours and wafting, feathery fins, leading them to be nicknamed The Jewels of the Orient. This one is an iridescent, electric-blue veiltail.

Upside-down Catfish (*Synodontis nigriventis*) are found in the Central Congo basin of Africa and are notable because they swim upside down. Tremendous fun to watch! They have been admired for countless centuries: pictures of them have been found in ancient Egyptian art. They adapted to swimming upside down in order to feed on insects on the surface of the water. To get an idea of what one looks like in the wild (or in ancient Egyptian art), turn the page upside down.

Orange Clownfish live symbiotically with anemones. These protect the clownfish from people who want to fry them (or other predators) and, in return, the fish groom the anemones and bring oxygen to them by swimming about. Their bold colouring is strikingly attractive: vibrant orange with three blue-white bands edged with a thin black border. This one is actually a false-clownfish. It has an extra 11th spine on its back; regular clownfish have only 10. That's how you tell them apart. (You can't do that here obviously, because this is a fillet).

FIVE GO
FACT FINDING ON
FORMOSA

Dick – likes cake and fighting and funambulism

Anne – likes the sort of things girls like, but not girls like George

Georgina – likes to be called 'George' and is a bit of a tomboy

Julian – would like to be an actuary or an exotic dancer

... and not forgetting Timmy the dog!

Formosa is a Fabulous Island in the Thames just brimming with "F"s and we're out to spot every one. Here we are at the "Tarry Stone" in Cookham which doesn't begin with an "F".

But how will we find Formosa? Julian has spotted a clue. "Why don't we follow this clearly marked Footpath? Come on, Timmy!"

But what's this? George is flummoxed by a mysterious sign. "Surely Heidegger conjectured there is no such thing as nothing? This really is jolly confusing."

But despite this logical inconsistency we decided to go on. The first "F" we find is... our Feet! "We'll need them to get to Formosa," says Dick, with no apparent irony.

Formosa, it turns out, is Full of Fruity Food. George decides to try what looks like a crab apple. "Hedgehogs like rolling in crab apples," George reminds us.

Oh Fiddlesticks! George has gone into anaphylactic shock which sounds like it should have an "F" in it but doesn't. Fortunately Dick knows First Aid.

George has made a Famous recovery and we're back on the hunt for "F"s. Flint! - the state gemstone of Ohio - Fascinating.[1]

Anne has found a Feather. "Look at me, Julian, I'm demonstrating the language of the Fan! This means 'lend me a Fiver!'"

Dick wants to go Fishing, but fears he might be committing a Felony if he does. Frightening.

"Come on, boys," cries Anne. "I fancy a spot of Feaguing!" But there are no eels to be found anywhere.[2]

"I say, Julian, is that a Filthy Fag in your Face?" "F*** off, Dick. 73% of the population of Manila smoke. If it's good enough for them it's jolly well good enough for me."

1. A man told us that flint was harder and sharper than steel, not bad considering it's actually made of dead sponges.
2. Apparently feaguing is an old term for sticking a root of ginger or a live eel up an animal's backside to make it perky.

FIGHT! "Stop!" cries Anne. "Aren't you boys aware that Pope Urban II expanded the 'Truce of God' (an edict which outlawed fighting) to last from Wednesday night to Monday morning, and it's only Thursday!"

The Fury is soon Forgotten however and we all settle down to a Feast. With lashings of ginger beer, of course. "Aristotle believed candied ginger gave men erections," quips George.

Dick eats a bit like a Foreigner. "Here's something else a bit Foreign," quips Dick. "In French, *un biscuit* is not a biscuit at all but a cake. A sponge cake, to be precise. A biscuit in the English sense is *un biscuit sec*."

Anne has found a forked stick. "If only dowsing wasn't such a bucketful of unproven arse-gravy," she sighs, delicately.

George is one of a rare group of "grass-spotters." "Look! Fescue, a genus of around 300 species of perennial tufted grass belonging to the family Poaceae," she squeals with delight.[3]

"My, it's hot. I Fancy I might Float, like most species of Ctenophores," hazards George.[4] "No, George!" cries Anne. "There are boys around. Cover your modesty!"

"Why should it always be the boys who have the Fun?" cries George.

But on Formosa no-one can be Fed up for long and soon we're all Frolicking across a Field.

It's time to say Farewell to Formosa. Thanks for showing us all your "F"s. They were great! What stories we'll have to tell when we get back home.

---

3. George should be careful. Some fescues carry a fungus which can cause weight gain, rough coat, panting and high rectal temperatures.
4. Ctenophores are a special type of fast-breeding hairy jellyfish. One species called 'the Monster' has destroyed all the fish in the Black Sea.

As I was going to QI

by Phill Jupitus

As I was going to QI

I met a man called Stephen Fry,

Alan Davies followed on,

Pursued by artist Jasper Johns,

After whom a circus bear

Then penguins eating
conference pears

Chewbacca with a ping-pong bat,

Some meerkats
wearing party hats,

A mighty horseman, name of Lars

A Dalek juggling Marmite jars,

A cow in an MCC tie,

How many were going to QI?

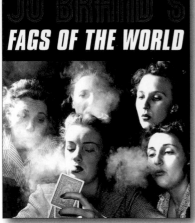

JO BRAND'S
FAGS OF THE WORLD

The fags elderly beagles long for.

Made in the Ukraine, but sensibly not smoked there.

Old fags for old lags.

Emphysema here we come!

What sort of wood do you want your coffin made of sir?

For thin scary teachers.

For thin scary pupils.

Easily concealed in the operating theatre.

Smoked by Joan Collins lookey-likeys.

Smoked by Joan herself.

South Korean fags North Koreans can only dream of.

Gold-coloured to piss off the North Koreans.

Will bring up a lung with your first toke.

Can use one to poke your lung back in.

Swanky yet wanky.

Popular with girls who like pictures of flowers.

Popular with asthmatic girls who like pictures of flowers.

The perfect fag to smoke in church.

Not a lucky strike for your lungs.

Makes your breath smell like faeces.

For weirdos who like beige.

For the cowboy with cancer.

Japanese, not mild and there aren't seven in a pack.

You are not allowed to mention them in Monte Carlo.

The Malaysian Coffin Nail.

Over a hundred years old, unlike its smokers.

Bafflingly called Los Angeles Blast.

Perfect for making Yorkshire pudding with.

Originally made with caustic soda, so shove one down your drain or your husband to freshen them up.

Popular with chain smoking MPs.

Popular with chain smoking lady MPs.

Slim and weak like an oiled seabird.

Probably smoked by God.

Actually God probably smokes these.

Certainly not these.

Packet design by an acid casualty.

Usually only smoked as a bet.

Make you very intelligent.

They should pay you to smoke these.

Dullest fag in the world.

Its very tedious little brother.

Its enormously emotionally disturbed maiden aunt.

Designed for young professional women like me.

Named after the famous anorexic tennis player.

The medieval sex offender of the fag world.

80

Does my corpse look big in this? | German über fags. | You won't be able to run to the shop for a packet of these. | Worth a whack from the headmaster. | These will help you get fitter, but only if you throw them away. | Made out of old settees. | Made out of young settees.

Not to be confused with Dabitoff. | Dead posh fags which will make you dead. | Shroud matching not a problem. | Strong fags smoked in Hungary. | Strong fags smoked when you're hungry. | The Samurai's choice. | The Geisha's choice.

Popular with asthmatic girls who like pictures of flowers and God forbid, pink as well the silly cows. | Very thin ones for very thin ones. | Symbolises luxury… my arse. | The original gasper. | Silly little fags with attitude. | The perfect fag to smoke after you've shagged your best friend's husband. | The perfect fag to stub out on a hoodie.

You are allowed to mention them in Monte Carlo but only at the weekends. | You are allowed to mention them in Monte Carlo but only if your child is called Givenchy. | The perfect accompaniment to Complan. | Thin and green like snot. | The probation officer's fag of choice. | The supply teacher's fag of choice. | The probation officer who wants to be a supply teacher's fag of choice.

A big packet for someone with a big packet. | A small packet for someone with a small packet. | A pointy packet for someone with a pointy packet. | 'Call this Mister'. | George Bush can't read this. | Germans love 'em and I love Germans! | Smoked by Poles and some Planks.

Make you very pretty. | Tasty and satisfying… unlike John McCririck. | An anagram of 'meals.' | Smoked by teenagers who can't spell. | The Caretaker's fag | Soft enough to smoke anally. | Rarely found in the pockets of builders.

The ballet dancer's fag of choice… although people often smoke a ballet dancer by mistake. | Popular in smaller branches of Debenhams. | Rhymes with chest and will get you wheezing. | Smoke West in your best vest, sex pest. | Perfect after a fight on the beach. | Often left in the machine. | A cunt of a fag. (Just checking you made it to the end.)

FRANCE
by Clive Anderson

France is a beautiful country, conveniently located just a few miles across the English Channel from Kent.

It boasts a wide range of stunning land and seascapes: a long stretch of Atlantic coastline, miles of Mediterranean beaches, a portion of Alps, half of the Pyrenees and a variety of other spectacular mountains, gorges and rivers. It is the most visited country on Earth.

The French people produce fine wines and even finer foods and have a high reputation in art, music, literature, philosophy and science.

Given all that, naturally we have spent most of the last thousand years waging war with them.

So engrained is the attitude of Anglo-French hostility that during the Crimean War when Britain and France were on the same side fighting Russia, the British commander Lord Raglan persisted in referring to the enemy (the Russians) as the 'French'.

And in 1944, wanting to bolster British morale in the final stages of the war against Germany, the government funded Laurence Olivier's film version of Shakespeare's *Henry V*, featuring England's glorious victory over the French (our allies in 1944) at Agincourt in 1415.

In recent years, France has enjoyed a poor reputation for military prowess in the English-speaking world. If you searched for 'French military victories' Google used to ask you, 'Do you mean French military defeats?' Homer Simpson - or was it George W. Bush? - called the French 'cheese-eating surrender monkeys'. This might be based on the French disinclination to support the invasion of Iraq in 2003 but is more likely harping back to the Second World War when French forces resisted the German advance for only 6 weeks before their government collaborated with the German occupation. As was said at the time:

Q: *Why do French roads have trees planted alongside them?*
A: *Because German soldiers like to march in the shade.*

And of course, at the beginning of the 19th century, the great French war leader Napoleon Buonaparte was defeated by Britain (and her allies) at Waterloo and Trafalgar, and by the Russians (and their winter) in Moscow.

Despite all this, the French military track record is actually rather better than the selective memory of Britain (and America) might suggest.

1066 BATTLE OF HASTINGS

This, the most famous English defeat in history, is remembered as a victory for the Normans rather than the French. King Harold and the English nearly won, but were beaten in the end by fixture build-up, having had to fight against the Norwegians at Stamford Bridge only a couple of weeks before. Plus William the Bastard used typically sneaky, continental tactics. His troops fought on horseback instead of riding to battle, getting off their horses and fighting on foot like proper Englishmen.

But, let's face it, Normandy was (and is) part of France. Contemporary documents from the *Anglo-Saxon Chronicle* to the Bayeux Tapestry refer to the invaders as French rather than Norman, and their arrival imposed a French-speaking aristocracy on England for hundreds of years.

One-nil to the French in anyone's language.

THE HUNDRED YEARS WAR, 1337-1453

In England, this conflict is largely remembered for its extraordinary length and for the glorious English victories at Crécy (1346), Poitiers (1356) and Agincourt (1415). However, the French also won important victories at Patay (1429) and at Castillon (1453), which are never mentioned in English history lessons but which brought the war finally to an end.

At the beginning of the war, English kings had pretensions to rule all of France, but by the end of it they possessed only the town of Calais. Though it had taken a while, it must count as another victory for France.

Not that the English were prepared to give up their claim on French territory just because they'd lost one small war. The symbol of France, the *fleur-de-lis* was only removed from the British Royal Coat of Arms nearly 350 years later, in 1801.

If you add in victories over the Moors in 701 (Tours); against Spain in 1603 (Rocroi); the British in America in 1781 (Yorktown); and Austria and Russia in 1805 (Austerlitz), the French batting average isn't so shabby. According to historian Niall Ferguson, out of a total of 168 important battles fought since 387 BC (which takes it back to some time before anything recognisable as 'France' quite existed), they have won 109, lost 49 and drawn 10.

THE AULD ALLIANCE

Until Great Britain came into existence, Anglo-French rivalry was very much an English-French thing (though the Welsh provided the 'English' bowmen at many important battles). Scotland had its own reasons for opposing England and so, in treaties from 1295 until the 16th century, it was as often as not allied to France, against England. The Auld Alliance, as it was known, was always old. It doesn't appear to have been called the New Alliance even in its early days. And it doesn't appear to have done Scotland very much good. Rather like the so-called Special Relationship between Britain and America, the smaller country puts the greater store on the deal, but gains less.

An Army of Scotland fought for France to great effect in the Hundred Years War. But France provided precious little help in the Scottish Wars of Independence at the beginning of the 14th century. The King of France even tried to get Robert the Bruce to go on a Crusade with him in 1309, which might have meant him missing the Battle of Bannockburn in 1314. And it was to honour the Auld Alliance that the Scots attempted their foolhardy invasion of England, leading to their bloody defeat at Flodden in 1513.

Later that century, again as part of the Auld Alliance, Mary, Queen of Scots also became Queen of France, but her abnormally short, stammering husband Francis II promptly died from an ear infection, less than 18 months after ascending the throne, aged 16. Mary went home to Scotland, where in due course she was arrested, imprisoned and executed in England.

Merci beaucoup.

FRENCH IN COURT

As mentioned above, the Normans introduced French to England and it was over 300 years before English once again emerged as the language of polite society and literature. Geoffrey Chaucer's *Canterbury Tales* (1387) was the first work of note in the mother tongue since 1066. The lawyers were even slower to catch on. Courtrooms clung to French long after even kings and queens had got round to communicating *en Anglais*. This meant that ordinary people couldn't follow what was going on in court – which is the way lawyers like it – and, if there was any opposition from the judges, it was probably because they would rather use Latin.

In 1362, a Statute of Edward III had required all court pleadings be in English. But the lawyers just wouldn't be told. As late as 1631, an ordinary criminal case is recorded as being in what amounts to courtroom Franglais, including the phrase: 'the prisoner ject un brickbat que narrowly missed'.

It wasn't until 1731, not far short of eight centuries since the Norman Conquest, that Parliament again enacted that English and not French should be used in all public legal proceedings. And this time the legislators got their way. (Though they did have to pass another Act in 1733 because they had forgotten to include Wales.) *Au revoir, enfin.*

FRENCH MILITARY TERMINOLOGY

Their business is war, and they do their business. RUDYARD KIPLING (1865-1936) in 1915

The British rightly pride themselves on their naval superiority, but this was largely born out of the certain knowledge that we would never win a war on the continent. Over its long history, the French army was usually the largest, best-equipped and most strategically innovative army in Europe. The language of modern warfare is French; all the following English words are of French origin; many even keep the original spelling.

arms, army, arsenal, attaché, artillery, attack, bandoleer, barracks, battery, bayonet, bombardier, brigade, cadet, camouflage, captain, carbine, colonel, combat, company, corporal, détente, division, dragoon, ensign, exercise, fort, fusilier, cavalry, charge, corps, epaulette, espionage, esprit de corps, garrison, general, grenade, grenadier, lieutenant, lance, marines, manoeuvre, melée, militia, military, mine, munitions, naval, offensive, ordnance, parachute, pilot, platoon, quarters, reconnaissance, recruit, regiment, ricochet, sabre, sergeant, soldier, sortie, standard, surrender, tent, terrain, trench, uniform, volley and volunteer.

It is well known with what gallantry the [French] officers lead and with what vehemence the troops follow.
GENERAL SIR WILLIAM NAPIER (1785-1860)

1. Franz Fanon (1925-61)

A psychiatrist, philosopher, author and revolutionary from the French colony of Martinique, his father was descended from African slaves. After France fell to the Nazis in 1940, he left the island and joined the Free French. Although decorated with the *Croix de Guerre*, he was forbidden to enter Germany with the victorious army because he was black. He dictated his greatest book *The Wretched of the Earth* (about Algeria's bitter struggle for independence) whilst dying of leukaemia.

2. Henri Farman (1874-1958)

Pioneering French aviator who was born in Paris, but was in fact English: his father was a foreign correspondent and he was christened Henry. Farman broke a number of early aviation records (including two world records for duration and distance) but there are two distinctions he will hold forever. In 1908, he became the first person in Europe to carry a passenger in an aircraft and the following year he was the pilot of the first aeroplane in the world to carry two passengers.

3. Felix François Fauré (1841-99)

Son of a small-time furniture maker, he rose to become President of France and died of apoplexy while having oral sex in his office with his mistress, 28 years his junior. Georges Clemenceau, who was born in the same year but outlived him by 30 years, commented: 'Il voulait être César, il ne fut que Pompée.' This had the deliberate double-meaning: 'he wanted to be Caesar, but ended up being Pompey' or 'he wanted to be Caesar but ended up being pumped'.

4. Gabriel Fauré (1845-1924)

The foremost French composer of his generation, his father sent him to music school in Paris aged nine, where he was considered so gifted that they charged no fee. Taught by Saint-Saens, he later taught Ravel. He is best known for his *Requiem* (which, he said, was not written for anyone in particular but just 'for the pleasure of it') and for *Berceuse* from his *Dolly Suite* (which was used by the BBC for 32 years from 1950 as the closing music for the children's radio show *Listen With Mother*).

5. Pierre Fermat (1601-65)

One of the greatest mathematicians of his day, Pierre Fermat was a lawyer and government official during the reign of Louis XIV. He was not a very good lawyer because he spent all his time on his hobby, but he rose to a senior position largely because many of his colleagues were struck down with the plague. Fermat himself was (wrongly) reported dead of the disease. His famous *Last Theorem*, whose proof he himself mysteriously failed to provide, was finally proven 328 years later.

6. Georges Feydeau (1862-1921)

Son of a beautiful Polish woman and rumoured to be the illegitimate son of Napoleon III, the master of French farce wrote the first of his 60 plays at the age of 7. Successful during his lifetime, but dismissed as lightweight, his works are continually revived and still widely performed today. A lover of high

living, Feydeau had a table permanently reserved at Maxim's in Paris. In 1918, he contracted syphilis and for the rest of his life gradually descended into madness.

7. Gustave Flaubert (1821-80)

Flaubert was born into a family of doctors but he himself was always ill, suffering from epilepsy and outbreaks of boils. 'I'm liquefying like an old Camembert', he said. World famous for his novel *Madame Bovary*, he achieved his first literary success at the age of 15 with a school essay on mushrooms. He had copied it off someone else and was later expelled. Although he had various mistresses, he lived with his mother until he was 51 and in later life was a compulsive frequenter of brothels.

8. Ferdinand Foch (1851-1929)

Marshal of France and commander of the allied forces at the close of the First World War, he was noted for 'the most original and subtle mind in the French army'. An able professor of military strategy, his famous saying was: 'Hard pressed on my right. My centre is yielding. Impossible to manoeuvre. Situation excellent. I attack.' Sacked after the Battle of the Somme he was later reinstated and went on to win the war. At the surrender, he refused to shake the hand of the German signatory.

9. Jean-Honoré Fragonard (1732-1806)

The son of a glove-maker and Court painter to Louis XV, Fragonard produced over 550 voluptuous and erotic paintings (not counting drawings and etchings). His daughter Rosalie was one of his favourite models. Later, he fell in love with his wife's 14-year-old sister. His career took a dive during the French revolution when the guillotine deprived him of most of his customers. Now feted as one of the all-time masters of French painting, he died in Paris in 1806 almost completely forgotten.

10. Anatole France (1844-1924)

The novelist Anatole France was born Jacques Anatole Thibault: he took his pseudonym from the name of his father's bookshop. He won the Nobel Prize for Literature in 1921, the year after the Vatican placed him on *The Index of Forbidden Books*. One of his mistresses, whom he had been cheating on for six years, died in 1910; a second one, whom he had deserted, killed herself in 1911, and his daughter Suzanne died in 1917. He also slept with his housekeeper, cheating on her too.

11. César Franck (1822-90)

Considered by many (including Franz Liszt) to be the greatest writer of organ music after J.S. Bach, Franck's first major public success as a composer did not come till he was 68 years old, the last year of his life. An innocent and absent-minded man, he scurried about Paris in an overcoat that was too large and trousers that were too short and died as a result of being run over by a bus. He lived most of his life in France but his mother was German and his father was a Belgian German.

THE F-UNNIES

'I'm not famine - I'm a supermodel.'

'I couldn't afford Bleak House.'

'I'm logged on to Imaginary Friends Reunited.'

*'You've got to see someone about
your incontinence.'*

Fragrance
by Kathy Phillips

Nothing is more memorable than a smell... or more difficult to describe.

As Diane Ackerman points out in her brilliant book *A Natural History of the Senses* (1990), most people, even if blindfolded, could instantly recognise the smell of a shoe shop, a church or a butcher's, but would be quite unable to describe the familiar aroma of a favourite chair or the inside of their own car. The vocabulary of smells is so small that we are forced to describe one in terms of another. Blood, it has been said, smells like dust and, according to Coleridge, a dead dog at a distance smells like elder flowers. But the fragrance of many things is completely unique: among them, penguins, which just smell... like penguins.

Essence of penguin has not (to my knowledge at least) ever been used in perfume but an amazing number of other things have. Not just the ones you might expect, like roses, jasmine, coconut or frangipani, but also baby powder, banana, butterscotch, cactus, coffee, dandelion, driftwood, grass, ginger, kiwi fruit, hazelnut, marshmallow, soil, spearmint and tomato. *Odeur 53* by Comme des Garçons has notes of oxygen, washing drying in the wind, nail polish, burnt rubber, tarmac and sand dunes. Tommy Hilfiger's *Tommy 10 For Men* cologne even claims to incorporate a whiff of Seattle rain.

include Christian Dior's *Dioressence* (1979), *Gucci No 1* (1972), Mary Quant's *Havoc* (1974) and *Monsieur Rochas* (1969).

Robert created *Calèche* in 1961 and for many years it was Hermès' best-selling women's fragrance (worn by, amongst others, Lady Mary Archer of 'fragrant' fame). He blended mandarin, orange blossom, jasmine,

PURE POISON ELIXIR Dior

© 2a for *Vogue* China

grass that smells of wet earth. It's used in many countries to control soil erosion. Ylang-ylang belongs to the magnolia family. Native to Indonesia and the Philippines and widely grown in the South Pacific, it is used as an aphrodisiac. It sounds like a created perfume in itself, with notes of rubber, custard, orange blossom and jasmine. Ylang-ylang is Malay for 'the flower of flowers' and Guerlain use so much of it that they have bought their own plantation on the Comoros Islands in the Indian Ocean.

For many centuries, there were just four key components of scent, none of them at all romantic. Musk is a red jelly found in deer-guts: it produces hormonal changes in any woman who smells it. Ambergris is a glutinous fluid found in the stomachs of sperm whales that protects them from the sharp beaks of the cuttlefish they swallow. It has a sweet, woody smell. Castoreum, a yellow secretion from the anal glands of mature beavers, has a whiff of leather. Civet is a honey-like goo exuded from the genitals of a nocturnal, fox-like, carnivorous, Ethiopian mongoose.

Nowadays, for understandable reasons, these grisly concoctions are reproduced in the laboratory, along with *calone*, an artificial 'sea breeze' aroma, and *cashmeran*, which is said to evoke the fragrance of cashmere. *Ozonic* compounds mimic the smell of the air after a thunderstorm. *Coumarin* is extracted from lavender, sweetgrass or the tonka bean (a cheap vanilla substitute) but is banned in the US as a food additive and is also used to make rat poison. But there remains an enduring connection between bottoms and perfume. The organic chemical *indole* is widely used in the perfume industry. It smells floral in low doses (and is present in many flowers, such as jasmine and orange blossom), but at high concentrations it smells like shit. Indole is found in human faeces.

Perfumes are the feelings of flowers.
HEINRICH HEINE* (1797-1856)

Scientists say that smell was the first of the senses to evolve. When primitive jellyfish began to develop brains, these actually began as buds on their olfactory organs. We think, as Diane Ackerman puts it, because we smelled.

People who create perfumes are known in the trade as 'noses'. For example, Jacques Polge became the 'nose' of Chanel in 1978 and Loc Dong was the nose behind Vera Wang's *Bouquet* (2008). *Le nez* responsible for *Calèche* was Guy Robert, the former president of the French Society of Perfumers, whose other hits

lily of the valley, rose, gardenia, iris, sandalwood and cedar with bergamot, oakmoss, vetiver and ylang-ylang.

What are these last four mysterious ingredients? Bergamot is an inedible variety of bitter orange present in the distinctive flavour of Earl Grey tea. Oakmoss (the more poetic-sounding *mousse de chêne* in French) is a kind of lichen. When it grows on oak trees it has a sharp, woody, slightly sweet smell; on pines it smells like turps, which some perfumers like a drop of. Vetiver (also known as khus khus) is a

The fragrance always remains in the hand that gives the rose.

CHINESE PROVERB

MEN! SPLASH IT ALL OVER! GET THE EDGE WITH ESTÉE LAUDER'S **DONALD TRUMP, THE FRAGRANCE**, A MELANGE OF EXOTIC WOODS, BLACK BASIL, MINT AND CUCUMBER.

*One thing eluded me.
I never managed to capture
the smell of honeysuckle.*

FRANÇOIS COTY* (1874-1934)

Headspace Technology, the newest form of perfume extraction, allows the scent of a living plant, flower, fruit or herb to be captured without having to damage it. For the first time, fragrances such as lilac, gardenia, violet and lily (known as 'the perfumer's despair') can be collected without destroying the plants. A single bloom, still attached at the roots, is placed in a bell jar through which a neutral gas is passed, acquiring the flower's vapour. Analysis of this gas enables the perfumer, using organic and synthetic ingredients, to reconstitute the perfume exactly.

Leather results from tanning, a disgusting and malodorous job that involves kneading animal skins with a mixture of human urine, dog dung and dissolved animal brains. Such foul odours inevitably lingered on the finished product. When Catherine de' Medici (1519-89) went to France at the age of 14 to marry the boy who would become King Henry II, she brought with her a whole host of ideas new to the French - including eating with a fork, corsets, ballet, high-heeled shoes and most importantly gloves scented with jasmine. These quickly became all the rage, to such an extent that the glove-making trade (huge in the 16th century) eventually transformed itself almost entirely into perfume manufacturing. Catherine's retinue included her personal perfumer, a sinister figure called René le Florentin. In his laboratory, connected to her quarters by a secret passage, he devised cunning new perfumes and medicines and he was also an expert in the use of poisons. His speciality was to send toxic gloves as gifts to the Queen's many enemies, including the pair said to have done for Jeanne d'Albret, mother of the future Henry IV.

*Heine was a poet and a German Jew; Coty was a Corsican fascist and newspaper baron (as well as a perfumer), born Joseph Spoturno. A shared passion for fragrance transcends both time and politics.

FRAGRANT FACTS

- Perfume smells strongest just before a storm.

- Cleopatra's ship had perfumed sails.

- Louis XIV decreed that a new perfume be invented for him every day.

- At the court of Louis XV, doves were drenched in different scents and released at banquets.

- The sweat of schizophrenics smells different to that of other people.

- Doctors use their noses to aid diagnosis. Typhus smells of mice, the plague of over-ripe apples and measles of freshly plucked feathers.

- 2 million Americans have *anosmia* - the inability to smell anything at all.

- A *factice* is a perfume bottle (sometimes giant size) made for display only: the contents aren't actually perfume.

Fletcher Christian, THE BOUNTY MUTINEER

In 1789, Acting Lieutenant Fletcher Christian led a mutiny against Lieutenant William Bligh, aboard the *Bounty*, a ship sent to Tahiti to collect breadfruit trees for cultivation as cheap food for slaves in the West Indies. The story of the mutiny is well known, thanks to Hollywood films, and countless books. But this most famous of Fletchers deserves to be remembered for more than just his rebellion...

ADRIAN TEAL fecit

Fletcher was at school with William Wordsworth. They both attended Cockermouth Free Grammar School in Cumbria.

Daffs again, eh, Wordsworth? D-Minus!

Nature table

Byron wrote the first dramatic poem about Fletcher and the mutiny, 'The Island' in 1823 (Don't bother reading it; it's terrible: full of unconvincing 'Awake, bold Bligh! the foe is at the gate!' kind of stuff.) Byron's grandfather, John 'Foul-weather Byron', had sailed with Philip Carteret, the man who discovered Pitcairn Island on his circumnavigation of the globe in 1766. Fortunately for Fletcher and the mutineers, he had charted its position wrongly, allowing them to make an island home safe from British justice. Their descendants still live there – somewhat controversially – today. The island was named after Midshipman Robert Pitcairn who first spotted it. His father, John Pitcairn, was a Royal Marine officer during the American Revolution, and his skirmish with the colonial militia in 1775 – the infamous Battle of Lexington – was the first engagement of the War of Independence.

Before stumbling across Pitcairn Island, Fletcher Christian discovered Rarotonga in the Cook Islands, and introduced the orange tree. Orange juice has been one of its most important exports.

Fletch's ORANGE JUICE

Fletcher ran the *Bounty* democratically and this continued once the mutineers and their Tahitian wives had landed on Pitcairn. By 1838, the islanders, now reconciled with the Crown, had enshrined a constitution that not only gave women equal rights to vote 90 years before their British counterparts but also made Pitcairn the first place under British jurisdiction to insist on compulsory schooling for both boys and girls. When Fletcher's Tahitian-born wife died in 1841 she did so having enjoyed more rights than most women in history.

'A painted ship upon a painted ocean'

The poetic connections didn't end with Byron. Many scholars think Fletcher was the inspiration for Samuel Taylor Coleridge's 'The Rime of the Ancient Mariner' (1799), since the mutineer is mentioned in one of the poet's notebooks. Coleridge certainly helped Mary Russell Mitford, with her Christian-related poem, 'Christina, The Maid of the South Seas' of 1811.

Midshipman Pitcairn says he's spotted uncharted land over there to the west of us...

That's the east, Captain...

Shut it, Byron...

Fletcher's family was well connected. Two cousins were bishops, another was Lord Chief Justice, and one was friendly enough with George Washington to marry his granddaughter. Yet another, John Christian Curwen, MP, owned Belle Isle in the middle of Lake Windermere. Fletcher's brother, Charles, was also involved in a mutiny while serving as Ship's Surgeon aboard the East Indiaman *Middlesex* in 1787. Fletcher's eldest son was called Thursday October Christian after his date of birth. In later years, when the crew of a passing ship politely explained that Fletcher had cocked up with regard to the international dateline, the son changed his name to Friday October Christian.

HOLLYWOOD HISTORY...

This is what you call a Lethal Weapon, Gibson!

He's gonna make me an offer I can't refuse!

ATOLL FOR SALE

Fletcher has been portrayed on screen by the Hollywood heart-throbs, Errol Flynn, Clark Gable, Marlon Brando and Mel Gibson, and in a naff stage musical by twinkle-eyed warbler David Essex. For the Brando version, white sand was imported to the location from the USA, because the black beaches of Tahiti didn't fit in with the audience's preconceptions about tropical islands. Brando bought the nearby Tetiaroa coral atoll after filming ended, marrying the Tahitian woman who played his lover, and named his baby son 'Christian'.

Bligh is a W⚓

BOUNTY BARS

CENSORED

The real Fletcher Christian didn't quite measure up to the matinée idol image. After the mutiny, Captain Bligh wrote a physical description to help the would-be captors at the Admiralty, describing him as having a 'star tattooed on the left breast and tattooed on the backside — his knees stand a little out and he may be called a little bowlegged. He is subject to violent perspiration, and particularly in his hands so that he soils anything he handles.' This condition was probably *hyperhidrosis*, which can be cured today by injecting the world's most toxic protein *botulinum* (also known as Botox) into the sweat glands. Fletcher was very fit: his party-piece was to put two ship's barrels side by side, stand in one, and then jump into the other.

So if he didn't look like Clark Gable, what *did* he look like?

No portrait of Fletcher Christian survives, so it seemed an interesting idea to research contemporary descriptions and track down portraits of the Christian clan, to help with family resemblance. Hairstyles and uniforms of the period were also studied before approaching the anatomically trained portrait artist, John Luce Lockett. He used these findings to produce the likeness you see here.

91

hammer of the god Thor. In early Christian and Byzantine art it was called the *gammadion*, gammadion cross or *crux gammata* because it can be made from four Greek capital gammas (G). It occurred among the Maya in South and Central America, and in North America amongst the Navajo. In India, to this day, the swastika is the most widely used symbol of auspiciousness in Hinduism, Jainism and Buddhism.

19. To broadcast the powerful suggestion to the rest of us that telepathy does not exist.

20. Sitting.

21. Shakerism: her name was Ann Lee.

22. Once – or twice if you count the original declaration of papal infallibility in 1870. Pope Pius XII issued an infallible statement in 1950 regarding the Assumption of the Blessed Virgin Mary (ie that she was transported body and soul to heaven).

F FOLK

23. The romantic smuggling novel *Moonfleet* (1898).

24. Cuthbert.

25. Cyd Charisse. Cyd was a childhood nickname: her brother couldn't pronounce 'Sis'. She was married to Nico Charisse, a dancer.

26. C.S. Forester.

27. Jean Henri Fabre (1823-1915). He devoted his whole life to the study of insects, carefully and beautifully describing and illustrating them in book after book, but he was 84 years old before anyone noticed. A poverty-stricken schoolteacher in provincial France, Fabre was a gifted and self-taught amateur entomologist who, on the publication of his last book, *Souvenirs Entomologiques*, suddenly achieved both literary and scientific world-renown. Scientific societies in London, Brussels, Stockholm, Geneva and St Petersburg elected him to membership and the French government gave him an annual pension. All students of insect behaviour, of comparative psychology and of experimental biology are indebted to him.

28. The White Cliffs of Dover. *Foraminiferans* are a form of zooplankton (tiny marine creatures from the Greek for 'wandering animals'). They live in shells made of the same stuff as limestone, marble and chalk. They manufacture these themselves by drawing calcium carbonate from the surrounding seawater. The sticky protoplasm of the *foraminiferan* flows in and out of holes in the shell to catch food. The holes or pores are what give the animals their name – *foramen* is Latin for a hole or orifice. As the animal outgrows its shell, it discards it and makes a new one.

THE F WORLD

29. He was neither Finnish nor a saint. He was English.

30. Only about 80% of it. Under French law, the French possessions of French Guiana in South America, Guadeloupe and Martinique in the Caribbean and Reunion in the Indian Ocean are as much part of France as Paris. By this definition, the total area of 'France' (including inland water) is 643, 427 sq km. Geographical (or metropolitan) France is only 547, 030 sq km. The 2.5 million inhabitants of the so-called 'DOM-TOM' (overseas departments and territories) are full French citizens.

31. Dutch. It means 'lemon'. The Citroen were a Dutch Jewish émigré family, who added the diaresis (the two dots over the 'o') to their name to make it classier.

32. The five islands in the Netherlands/Dutch Antilles (Curaçao, Bonaire, Sint Eustatius, Saba and Sint Maarten), and Aruba, which separated from them in 1986, but remained within the Kingdom of the Netherlands. The Netherlands Antilles florin is usually called the guilder; since 1986, the Aruban currency is usually called the florin, but the two terms are interchangeable. 66% of the Aruban population speak Papiamento, a Spanish-Dutch-Portuguese-English dialect.

33. A thimble.

34. Fundy. The highest tides in the world occur near Wolfville, Nova Scotia in the Minas Basin in the Bay of Fundy between Nova Scotia and New Brunswick in Canada. The sea level can change as much as 16 m (45 ft) between high and low tide. At mid-tide, the amount of water travelling through the Minas Channel is equal to the combined flow of all the rivers and streams on Earth put together. The 14 cubic kilometres (14 billion ton/s) of seawater that flow into Minas Basin twice a day cause Nova Scotia to bend and tilt slightly under the strain.

35. FORFEIT: ANY PERCENTAGE EXCEPT 0
0% according to the UN Food and Agriculture Organisation. Guyana's rain forests have a similar level of biodiversity to those in the Amazon but, unlike Brazil's, they are not disappearing. Logging in Guyana is selective, with only 35 out of 1,000 tree species logged commercially. Because of Guyana's excellent record in forest management and conservation, the forests, ironically, are considered to have no value. Yet they seed rain that irrigates farmland as far away as the American Midwest, house thousands of species of plants and animals (including many rare ones) and store thousands of ton/s of carbon. The Iwokrama reserve in Guyana is 371,000 hectares in extent (roughly the size of Majorca). Trees are cut down at the rate of one per hectare per year and only from half of the reserve's total area. Iwokrama has recently signed a deal with British financiers Canopy Capital. They have 'valued' the forest at $20 per hectare. If this were a commercial proposition to store carbon, the deal would work out at $0.20 per ton/s. By comparison, BP is planning to spend $50-60 per tonne pumping carbon into disused oilfields in the North Sea.

FLORILEGIUM*

36. They were all cobblers. Stalin's and Hans Christian Andersen's mothers were both also washerwomen.

37. Teaching children to utter their first word.

38. FORFEIT: AMERICA/USA
The use of the word 'fall' or 'the fall' to mean autumn is commonly assumed to be an Americanism, but in fact it is found in the works of Elizabethan writers Michael Drayton (1563-1631), Thomas Middleton (1580-1627) and Sir Walter Raleigh (c 1554-1618). The expression was originally 'the fall of the leaf'. The earliest recorded use of 'fall' in this sense in English occurs in 1545 in *Toxophilus*, a treatise on archery by Roger Ascham (1515-68). Ascham's book was hugely popular, gaining him a royal pension of £10 a year. It was later taken as the model for *The Compleat Angler* by Izaak Walton.

39. The last Maltese falcon or Mediterranean peregrine (*Falco peregrinus brookei*). Gozo is the second largest island in the Maltese archipelago, after Malta itself.

40. The dragon that guards the treasure of the Nibelungen. It means 'Smith' in Norse, just as Cain, the first murderer, does in Hebrew.

[See the Effing Difficult Quiz, p. 43]

EFFING DIFFICULT ANSWERS

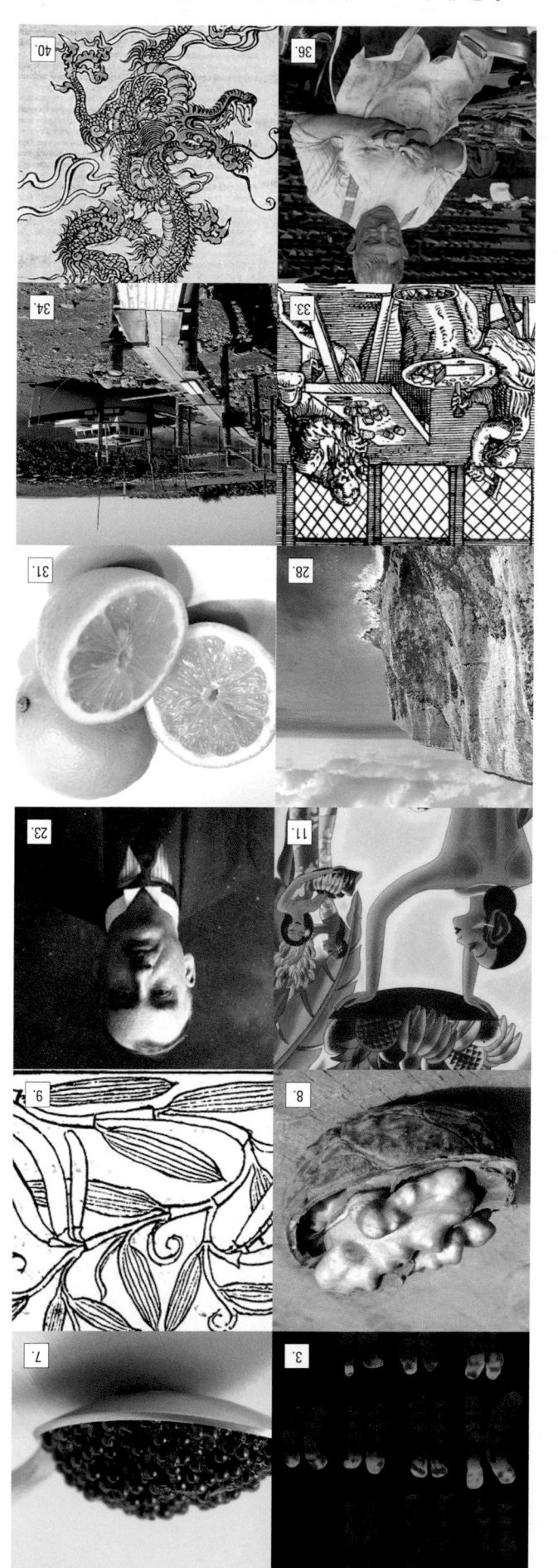

* *Florilegium* means literally 'a collection of flowers' in Latin, hence, an anthology (a word which also literally means 'collection of flowers', but in Greek).

F WORDS

1. 51 times. We've done the maths.
2. FORFEIT: PLANTS/ANIMALS
   The answer is neither: they have their own separate Kingdom – though they are thought to be more like animals than plants.
3. It has more chromosomes, 1,320, than any other living thing. Adder's Tongues are small strikingly inconspicuous plants less than 15 cm (6 in) tall. Each plant has just one smooth-edged, pointed, oval leaf. They look nothing like ferns and are easily mistaken for the seedling of a flower.
4. Fermentation.
5. The Old English name for the swastika.
6. Fulmars, also called tubenoses and stinkers, are large seabirds related to petrels. The name is from the Norse meaning 'foul gull'.
7. Pressed caviar.

FRUIT

8. Walnuts. (All nuts are fruit.) The taxonomic name for the walnut genus is *Juglans*, of the family *Juglandacaeae*. It is Latin for 'walnut' but it literally means 'the head of God's penis'. *Juglans* is an abbreviation for *Jovis glans* ('the glans of Jove') - Jove (or Jupiter) being king of the gods, and *glans* being Latin for the head of the penis, from its original meaning 'acorn', which it closely resembles.
9. Vanilla. Vanilla is a kind of orchid. The English word 'vanilla' comes from the Spanish *vainilla*, the diminutive of *vaina*, a sheath or scabbard, hence pod, husk or shell. Vaina is from the Latin *vagina* of which the original meaning was also sheath or scabbard. The word 'orchid' comes from the Greek *orchis*, meaning 'the testicles', plural of *orcheis*. Orchids are so called because of the shape of their roots.
10. FORFEIT: TOMATOES
    Walnuts. They were a fertility symbol and a rather painful form of confetti.
11. FORFEIT: HAWAII
    Thailand (11%), The Philippines (11%), Brazil (10%), China (10%), India (9%). Pineapple production varies from year to year, so any of these answers is acceptable. Hawaii, for many years the pineapple king, now produces less than 2% of the world's supply. Del Monte recently closed a factory there.
12. Strawberry. Strawberries are not fruit, they are 'false fruit' or pseudocarps. The actual fruit are the little white or brown specks that get stuck in your teeth.
13. FORFEIT: PRISONERS
    Monkeys, imported from Panama, were used to reduce labour costs. Each gang had a human foreman who set them loose in the orchards. They scampered up the trees, harvested all the plums as planned, and then ate the lot.
14. Lemon. 'Dribly' also has some lime in it.

FAITH

15. FORFEIT: ISLAM
    Mormonism. There are 5 times as many Mormons as there were in 1960.
16. Shinto. There are innumerable deities in Shinto, but the chief one is the sun goddess Amaterasu-o-mikami, 'the great shining goddess in the sky'.
17. The Jehovah's Witnesses: Jesus succeeded him. On taking command, he threw Satan and his wicked angels out of Heaven and down to earth. This is why things have become so unpleasant in the world since 1914.
18. Zoroastrianism. The swastika is an ancient and virtually universal symbol, which has been used all over the world from prehistoric times up to the present day, almost always representing prosperity and good fortune. It was a favourite sign on coinage in ancient Mesopotamia. In ancient Scandinavia, the left-handed swastika represented the

·FIBONACCI·F·F·I·B·N·C·FB·

Flourish

führer

flash

Fold

FIZZ

Ho+m²ul=a

fife

fart

ORWARD F

FLIP

FAT

LYING FISH

farce

feuillemorte

FAR

fetter

fluid

FAHRENHEIT

FLUCTUATE

foe

FRONT

FREUD

Fondle

94

BO·NN·CI·FOO·IBB·BCC·A

flood fingerprint fez

F·8·I FOOD flora

Fancy FLAT FOUCAULT

FIRE flexible

FAX INISTERRE

filibusterfilibusterfilibuster,

FLY TRAP fogey

FLOTSAM Fossil

fault Slummox FADE

FLAINT FELICID

Ye Daily Telegraph

MONDAY 18TH OCTOBER 1381
Free Advertisements of Sundry Kinds

Lord Mayor and Mercer to the King, Richard 'Dick' Whittington says *"I would probably still be sitting in a puddle of my own filth were it not for my MAGICAL CAT"*. Everybody knows it's impossible to improve yourself. No matter how hard you work or who you defer to the old phrase still holds true 'Once a peasant, always a peasant' - until now. Meet MAGICAL CAT. With MAGICAL CAT you can now aspire to better yourself in life. Imagine earning money and moving through society. Soon you'll be endowing grammar schools and leaving a SMALL FORTUNE to charity in the hope of preserving your greedy, mercenary soul from hell fire. And when you get back from a hard day counting money you'll be able to say *"Thanks MAGICAL CAT"*.

MAGICAL CAT – THERE'S NO OTHER EXPLANATION FOR IT!

PLEASE Rush me my MAGICAL CAT for the bargain price of TEN ENGLISH POUNDS. I am astonishingly gullible. Send money NOW to: The Richard Whittington Home for Stray Cats, Suthwerk, Nr London.

END PLAGUE MISERY NOW

Are there times when you wonder if the pestilence will ever go away? Now you can say 'bye-bye buboes' with our fabulous 'pomander'. Pomander is a revolutionary metal ball stuffed with leaves, sticks and other stuff probably proven to be effective against pestilence and **MUCH MORE**. Pomander is not only proof against all forms of miasmas and foul airs – it's also fun and fashionable. Pomander costs just **1 angel** – is your family worth it?

You Too Could Become a Writer – With the majority of the population ***WHOLLY ILLITERATE*** there's never been a better time to become a writer and with the new notion of 'printing', your words could literally reach hundreds. Writing everything from scurrilous pamphlets to pornographic chronicles can be exciting and rewarding and the **SCRIVENING SCHOOL** is with you all the way*. You will receive personalised tuition from a host of published authors (*G. Chaucer or W. de Worde*) and before long the farthings will come flooding in. *Full money-back guarantee if you can find us.*

"I just copied out a French fabliau and changed a few bits and now I'm considered the father of English literature – Brilliant!" G. Chaucer

Send a stamped addressed parchment for further details to: Wynkyn de Worde School of Scrivening, The Swan Tavern, St. Paul's Churchyard, London.
up to, but not including, arrest, torture and execution.

VACANCIES:

Why not become an anchoress? Being walled up alive can be more rewarding than you might think. In return for simple prayers and advice your community will feed you for free (terms and conditions may apply) and, when necessary, bury you in the hole you have spent your life excavating in the floor of your cell. Become an anchoress and really dig your own grave! Apply Julian of Norwich.

VACANCY: King of Poland. Owing to the unexpected running away of the previous incumbent a vacancy now exists for the position of Polish Monarch. Poland is a vibrant and

backward mediaeval state at the heart of a brutal theocratic Europe and the role of king requires an unusual combination of naivety and recklessness. With a history of unprovoked regicide, Poland will provide an exciting challenge for the successful applicant who, in return, can expect a handsome compensation package including a gloomy official residence and a full state funeral. *Previous applicants need not, and largely cannot, apply. Please fill in coupon for further details.*
YES PLEASE! I have what it takes to be the next King of Poland. I also have no next of kin.
Name:
Address:
Send to: "I want to be King", The Human Resources Manager, Kraków Castle, Kraków, Poland.

THOUGHT ABOUT NECROMANCY?

WE SINCERELY HOPE NOT. THE NATION OF ENGLAND OFFERS NECROMANCERS A VARIETY OF PAINFUL DEATHS DEPENDING ON SOCIAL STATUS. MINOR CLERICS AND LOCAL BUMPKINS CAN EXPECT ALL THE PAGEANTRY OF BEING HANGED, DRAWN AND QUARTERED IN FRONT OF A LIVELY AND ENTHUSIASTIC CROWD. THOSE OF A HIGHER STATION IN LIFE CAN LOOK FORWARD TO ANYTHING FROM A 'MYSTERIOUS DISAPPEARANCE' TO BEING BANISHED FOR LIFE TO THE ISLE OF MAN.

WANTED: Stale piss. Top prices paid by London fuller. Help keep the nobility smelling like a cess pit.

LUXURY TOURING HOLIDAYS

For years the idea of walking slowly and painfully to Canterbury on unmade roads in the company of drunks was little more than a DREAM for most peasants. Now even the humblest turnip-eater can join in the magic. Walking parties leave from the Tavern in Suthwerk every Monday. Tour includes brigands, insults and the chance to be WHOLLY DEFRAUDED by the monks of Canterbury on arrival. So why not come to Canterbury and have your own tale to tell? *Apply G Chaucer, Customs House, Newgate.*

LIMB LOSS?

Worried about unsightly limb loss? The Leper Hospital of St. Nicholas can help. Look years younger with one of our wooden legs, hand carved from old wood and, at a sufficient distance, almost indistinguishable from the real thing. Also just in – crutches!

Apply now for a free colour parchment to: The Hospital of St. Nicholas Beyond the Walls (actually quite a long way beyond the walls), York.

AFTERLIFE INSURANCE: Only the Holy Catholic and Apostolic church offers genuine PURGATORY afterlife insurance. Endow a chantry chapel, build a cathedral or even just give bread to the poor to earn *Remission of Sins* in Purgatory. Remember the prayers of the poor can save YOU from hell. No other religion offers this simple and convenient way to avoid DAMNATION. Just leave us your money and we'll do the rest, leaving you to really '*rest in peace*'. And remember, the more you leave us, the shorter your torment.

The Catholic Church **is** Purgatory!

DOMESTIC SITUATIONS

Serf required for busy manor. Must be willing t work to outmoded feudal concepts. Apply Th Abbot of St.Alban's, Dining Hall, St. Alban's Abbey

Executioner – Reliable and imaginativ executioner required by busy tyran Excellent rates of pay and exotic travel. Nc for the squeamish. *Apply Tamerlane, Khan of the Timurids, Royal Palace, Samarkand.*

££££ EARN Groats as a Pardoner £££ *Why slave under feudal tenure when you could b earning up to a groat a day – every day? Pardonin is easy to learn and fun to do. Your bishop wi provide you with all necessary materials – you ju have to go out and sell a little bit of heaven!*

FOR SALE

'The World Turned Upside Down' – rea John Gower's explosive new manuscript *Vo Clamantis* on why modern life is rubbis Available in all good scriptoria.

Sheep – one careful owne Some superficial damage All offers considered. *Apply Roger Lambkin.*

Magnificent moss-stuffed winkle-pickers Note – may not comply with your loc sumptuary laws. Check before buying *Symond the Cobbler.*

Village full of peasants, availabl individually or as a lot. Owing to move int sheep farming no longer required for lives o meaningless servitude. Not allowed to drow them so will give them to any suitable c unsuitable home, provided they don't com back. *Apply Richard of Cotesford, Tusmore.*

Hilarious tabards – 'My Other Cart is Cart', 'My Wife of Bath Went to Canterbur and All I Got Was This Lousy Tabard' an many, many more. Available in off-white onl As seen at the opening of Parliament. *Sen for full details to 'Tabardtastic', Gropecun Lane, London.*

LONELY HEARTS

FABULOUSLY UGLY YORKSHIR HARRIDAN (probably a witch) wltm gent parfait knight. **Apply Alison Gross**

Notts-based bandit seeks posh lass for fun in the fores **Apply R. Loxley, Sherwood.**

GAY KING GSOH REQUIRES TEEN BRIDE FOR SAKE OF APPEARANCES. **APPLY TOWER OF LONDON.**

When Adam Delved and Eve Span, Wh was then the Gentilman? With a third of the population dead there' never been a better time to think about career change. Ever wondered what it woul be like to lord it over your very own peasant Ever thought about dying in a different station in life to the one you were born into? Now yo can with my simple Manor Invasio Programme. I'll show you in three easy step how to (1) Destroy the manorial records tha bind you to the land; (2) Seize untenante property; (3) Bribe the local aristocracy t keep schtum. Or join me on Blackheat Common for our first seminar, featuring Wa Tyler and me, John Ball.

NOTE: *Written programme requires basic literacy.*

The *QI F Annual* was written, researched, illustrated and otherwise enhanced by Ronni Ancona, Clive Anderson, Rowan Atkinson, Jo Brand, Craig Brown, Derren Brown, Rob Brydon, Jimmy Carr, Tom Climpson, Stevyn Colgan, Mat Coward, Alan Davies, Cherry Denman, Ted Dewan, Chris Donald, Geoff Dunbar, Hunt Emerson, Stephen Fry, James Harkin, Tony Husband, Phill Jupitus, Roger Law, John Lloyd, Sean Lock, John Mitchinson, Ben Morris, Nick Newman, Molly Oldfield, Kathy Phillips, Justin Pollard, Anthony Pye-Jeary, David Stoten and Adrian Teal.

Designed by David Costa and Nadine Levy at Wherefore Art? Email david@whereforeart.com
Cover illustration: Adrian Teal

Editorial: Sarah Lloyd
Editorial Administrator: Liz Townsend

Picture research: Wherefore Art? with help from Mark Boutros, Will Elworthy, James Harkin, Caitlin Lloyd and Liz Townsend.

Photography: Jim Marks (www.marks.co.uk) for Rowan Atkinson's 'Furniture Masterclass' and the 'Foto Love Story'; Brian Ritchie (ritchiestills@btinternet.com) for the *QI* production photographs; Mark Boutros (markpaulboutros@hotmail.com) for 'Five Go Fact Finding on Formosa'; Harry Lloyd and David Costa for 'A Farrago of Fruit'; 2a for *Vogue* China, for 'Fragrance'.

The researchers for the *QI F Annual* were Mat Coward; James Harkin; John Lloyd; John Mitchinson; Molly Oldfield and Justin Pollard.

QI Logo design: Jules Bailey.

With thanks to Steve Colgan and Chris Hale for permission to adapt their 'Middenshire Chronicles' for 'Fakenham'; Sally Cooper for lashings of ginger beer and chocolate cake; Sarah Falk; The Groucho Club; Kate Kessling; Coco Lloyd; Ben Morris for the illustrations of Jimmy Carr; NASA; Oxfordshire County Council Museum Resource Centre at Standlake; Oscar Pye-Jeary; Jan 'Boris' Szymczuk; the *Daily Telegraph* for permission to use their logo, and all at Faber, especially Dave Watkins for his patience and support.

With special thanks to **HEAL'S** for permission to photograph Rowan Atkinson at their store in Tottenham Court Road, London.

Photo credits:
Bigstockphotos (www.bigstockphoto.com) for 'Form' and 'Fried Fish'
Corbis (www.corbis.com) for 'Fallacybuster' (figures); 'France' (man with onions); 'Effing Difficult Quiz';
'A Farrago of Fruit' (blossom); 'Funambulism' (background image, woman on a wire)
DK Picture Library (www.dkimages.com) for 'Falcon vs Ferret' (Falcon)
Getty Images (www.gettyimages.com) for 'Fallacybuster' and 'Fours' and 'Fives'
Mary Evans Picture Library (www.maryevans.com) for 'France'(group of soldiers) and 'Fairly Famous F Frenchmen'
PA Photos (www.paphotos.com) for 'Funambulism' (Philippe Petit)
Punchstock Picture Library (www.punchstock.com) for 'Falcon vs Ferret' (Ferret)
Rex Features (www.rexfeatures.com) for 'Football in Mouth'
Topfoto (www.topfoto.co.uk) for 'Jo Brand's Fags of the World' (title image)
V&A Images Victoria and Albert Museum (www.vandaimages.com) for 'Funambulism' (lion)

The answer is 'Smith'. The list is the top twenty surnames today in Vancouver, capital of the province of British Columbia in Canada. Smith is the eighth commonest name in the city.